A
MOONLESS,
STARLESS SKY

A
MOONLESS,
STARLESS SKY

ORDINARY WOMEN AND MEN
FIGHTING EXTREMISM IN AFRICA

ALEXIS OKEOWO

corsair

CORSAIR

First published in the US in 2017 by Hachette Books
First published in Great Britain in 2017 by Corsair

1 3 5 7 9 10 8 6 4 2

Photograph on p. 237 courtesy Tadej Znidarcic

A CIP catalogue record for this book
is available from the British Library.

ISBN: 978-1-4721-5371-5

Printed and bound in Great Britain by Clays Ltd, St Ives plc

Papers used by Corsair are from well-managed forests
and other responsible sources.

Corsair
An imprint of
Little, Brown Book Group
Carmelite House
50 Victoria Embankment
London EC4Y 0DZ

An Hachette UK Company
www.hachette.co.uk

www.littlebrown.co.uk

For my parents.

CONTENTS

AUTHOR'S NOTE

For the safety of certain individuals I interviewed, I have altered names or provided only first names.

PREFACE

I DIDN'T plan on becoming obsessed with Africa. But ever since taking a ten-month internship at a newspaper in Uganda after college, I have returned to the fascinating, unpredictable, and maddening continent again and again to report stories. Before moving to Uganda at the age of twenty-two, I had traveled to Africa just once: In elementary school, my Nigerian parents took my brothers and me to their country of birth for Christmas, and we shyly and awkwardly united with dozens of relatives we had never met. My parents had both ended up as college students in Alabama, where I grew up. We had all the comforts of Nigerian food, art, and music in my childhood home, but I didn't have a great interest in Africa. I was drawn more to the prospects of adventure.

I traversed Uganda, flying in tiny planes to the remote, arid northeast and the border with Sudan, and bungee jumping over the Nile River, all the while trying to figure out my relationship to its inhabitants. Feeling neither wholly American nor African, I had come to see myself as an outsider in both places, an observer at the fringes. It was a perspective that helped me learn to report with clarity. Five years after my internship in Uganda, I moved from Brooklyn back to Africa, this time to have a home base in Nigeria. It was then that I realized things had changed. After several years in and out of Africa, becoming familiar with so many of its cultures and parts, I no longer felt like an outsider. The continent had become a second home.

But as a novice reporter in Uganda, I initially approached my subjects—back then, primarily survivors of the civil war—with a mix of alienating emotions. Sympathy, for the suffering they had endured, which usually turned into pity, and a blend of disbelief and bewilderment that they had come through to the other side, mostly intact, still able to laugh and feel joy and express compassion for strangers.

I was writing 800-word news stories that didn't delve deeply into my subjects' lives, and they still felt foreign and incomprehensible. It took time to understand that what I was beginning to feel intimately—a kinship to Ugandans, a sense that we were far more alike than we were dissimilar—had to extend to how I undertook my reporting. If I wanted readers to understand that the people I interviewed were not that different from them, I needed to practice empathy when writing. That meant telling the stories of their lives, their likes and dislikes, their hobbies, the people they cared for. It meant conveying that I understood that I could have been a woman who had been disfigured by a rebel group had not it been for the fortune of my birthplace.

As my reporting deepened, the lives that interested me the most were the everyday, complicated Africans who were dealing with religious and cultural fundamentalism, state failure, and conflict, people who were grappling with their countries and trying to push them forward. What does resistance mean in the fight against extremism in Africa? There is the obvious profession of an activist: someone who has devoted her life to a cause. That cause usually swallows activists whole, dominates their lives. Activists can stage protests and sit-ins; they can also, in radical cases, take up arms. Liberty, that precious, delicate right, is fleeting in so much of the world. Sometimes it is there for you to take and enjoy; other times it suddenly and violently disappears, as if it never existed in the first place. But there are always people who go looking for that freedom, even at personal risk. They are not only activists and vigilantes, but also ordinary people. I became interested in subtler forms of resistance, ways of fighting that are not as easy to notice. Preserving your way of life amid extreme situations is also a vital struggle. That can mean continuing to live in your house, going to work, seeing your friends, dancing, playing sports and music, being as free as you know you deserve to be. It can also mean loving who you want, no matter who that person is, and keeping your family together.

What are the ethics of resisting? When extreme circumstances are forced upon a person, what is she allowed to do to survive? Can she commit apostasy as a religious person, or kill a relative? The answers are complex, possibly unknowable. The idea of survival becomes hazy: It can mean more than just staying alive; it can mean leading the life she feels entitled to have. And in order to do that, the morals she was taught, that she has long lived by, could shift and mutate into something she no longer recognizes. They could change because she believed she was fighting for good, or at least for her right to have a good, sane life, and, along the way, she had to resort to actions she would have never committed in the past. They could change because, when extreme circumstances overtook her life, subverted what she knew and held dear, resorting to radical measures was the only way to resist, and to live.

The four stories in *A Moonless, Starless Sky* all deal, in some way, with extremism within Christianity and Islam. But there are many types of extremism, in the spheres of gender and sexuality, nationalism, and race. These stories are only a few windows into what is happening in Africa. And it is revealing that the women and men fighting back are Christian and Muslim, too, and often fighting within their religions for the principles in which they believe.

I don't have much experience with resisting extremism in my own life. But I do know what it is like to live in a culture of extremes, as a black girl who grew up in the Deep South in the 1990s. Within days of moving to Alabama, a white woman shouted "Nigger!" at my father, my brother, and I as we drove past her car at a gas station.

My father immediately reversed the car and pulled into the station to ask the woman what, exactly, she had said. She had nothing to say after that. A pack of white boys at my high school in Montgomery, home of the Civil Rights Movement, wore T-shirts, sweaters, whatever they could find, emblazoned with the Confederate flag. I went to an academically rigorous school and had white and black friends, but my relationships with my white classmates always had a terminal boundary, past which lay weekend sleepovers and house parties that I couldn't join because it just wasn't done. And so, I became used to the extreme polarity of race where I lived, darting between each end with frequency, but never feeling free to jump off one with abandon.

For years, my family faithfully attended an evangelical church that tried to do good works in minority communities. One day, before an upcoming election, the pastor announced a list of right-wing politicians he wanted the congregation to vote for, even though they had no record of representing his black, working- and middle-class parishioners' interests. He was trying to curry favor with the city's political elite. When we left the church after the pastor's hypocrisy was exposed, it did feel like a win. That is the thing about fighting extremism—each victory, tiny and large, can feel monumental.

PART ONE

UGANDA

An LRA love Story

THE MOONLESS, starless sky was bright the evening Eunice met Bosco in the forests of southern Sudan. The year was 1996, and Eunice had been kidnapped two weeks earlier from a school in a town called Aboke, in northern Uganda, by men who called themselves the Lord's Resistance Army. Founded by a young man named Joseph Kony in 1987, the LRA was raiding villages in Uganda's north and abducting children while routing the Ugandan army. Eunice was a thoughtful girl of fifteen with inquisitive eyes and closely cropped hair, and she had been visiting her older sister at a girls' boarding school when rebels surrounded the building. The men, who were really boys if you looked at them closely, tied the girls together with rope and forced them to trek through the forests of northern Uganda, on the way to Sudan, for over a week while they cooked, did laundry, and fetched water for them. Eunice was frightened and exhausted. She was still wearing the blue cotton skirt, her best one, and the matching blouse that she had thought would impress her sister's friends. Eunice wanted to attend their school one day, too, be among these accomplished girls, and she had hoped to show them that she could fit in, be smart and interesting, dress like they did.

The girls eventually crossed into Sudan and stopped in an area of tall grass and thick, looming trees. More men emerged, including Kony. Rebels began plucking girls from the group, choosing the prettiest ones first. Eunice watched with a swelling sense of dread. There was nowhere to run. They were everywhere. A boy named Bosco, who looked like he was no older than seventeen, appeared in front of her. He was wearing rain boots, a green military uniform that slouched on his thin frame, and a matching cap over bushy hair. Another rebel, who seemed like he was one of the men in charge, nudged Bosco closer toward Eunice and told him, "This will be your wife."

Eunice was still; she felt paralyzed. She had nearly just died when the Ugandan military emerged out of nowhere and fired gunshots at the rebels as they led the girls through the bush, and death, she thought, would make more sense than what was happening to her right now.

"You're blessed that you've come to me. We thought that you girls might refuse us. You'll be okay," Bosco said to her.

Bosco was nineteen. Three years earlier, the LRA had also kidnapped him and trained him to be a soldier. Bosco had felt himself become hardened to the killings and kidnappings he was ordered to carry out. But when he first saw Eunice, he fantasized of a new family that would replace the siblings and mother he had lost. He imagined that he had finally found someone to trust. She was the most beautiful girl he had ever seen.

Eunice was repulsed. *I have no interest in this man,* she thought. *How will I get to know him when I absolutely do not want to be with him?* Bosco led her to a tent constructed of tree branches with a tarp laid on top, a fragile bush hut, where they would begin the rest of their lives.

Uganda was a sheet of green unfurled over slopes and through forests that stretched to its borders with South Sudan and the Democratic Republic of the Congo, and sometimes it extended over those boundaries, too. The range of greens within a single field looked like a child poured buckets of every hue of green paint into the plants, the trees, the bushes. There was also red dirt, and redder mud, but it was the green that stood out. The cities were always under construction, choked with pollution, traffic, and new malls and apartment complexes. In the northern countryside, above the Nile River, the green still meant fertile land and roots, that what once belonged to your ancestors was now yours to bring to fruition. It could mean both struggle and fortune. The green never felt completely familiar; there was a reason people left so much of it intact in the great expanses between their houses and the houses of their neighbors, and why, no matter how much intruders tried to tear it down, it sprang back up again. To the people of northern Uganda, the green did two more things: It sheltered those who needed a home and camouflaged those who sought to destroy the very idea of it.

Called the "Pearl of Africa" by former British prime minister Winston Churchill, Uganda won its independence from Britain in 1962 after seventy-two years as its colony. A landlocked teardrop in East Africa, the country has a population of almost 40 million people and multiple ethnic identities that the British exploited as they divided and ruled. The British army recruited mostly from the Acholi ethnic group in northern Uganda, while many of the Baganda in the south worked in business or civil service. After independence, these groups competed for jobs, land, and power. The new nation quickly became beset by a series of violent coups and armed rebellions.

Milton Obote, Uganda's first postindependence prime minister, was from the Lango region in the north and drew support from the Lango and Acholi groups. He formed an alliance with the Baganda in the south, but soon dissolved the constitution and declared himself president, beginning a dictatorship that terrorized opponents and stole from the national coffers. A general named Idi Amin from the northwestern Kakwa group overthrew Obote to begin his own brutal regime that disappeared and killed thousands of people, and purged Lango and Acholi soldiers from the military.

When forces within Uganda and from neighboring Tanzania forced Amin into exile, Obote reemerged to win the 1980 election. His return was not smooth.

Guerilla leader Yoweri Museveni accused him of rigging the race, and Museveni's rebel National Resistance Army, made up largely of southerners, waged war against Obote. The people of Uganda were tired. They had endured bloodshed and a never-ending turnover of despotic leaders, and were desperate for stability. But more coup plans, as always, were brewing.

General Tito Okello, an Acholi, overthrew Obote. Okello signed a peace deal with Museveni's rebels at the end of 1985, but Museveni seized power a month later anyway. He was still in power in 2017. Once Museveni assumed office, soldiers and government officials loyal to Obote and Okello fled back north. They were afraid of retaliation at the hands of the new government, which was angry about massacres Obote's army had committed in central Uganda of residents who supported Museveni. Acholis watched as Museveni's army then committed murder and rape and seized land and cattle, in their own communities, under the guise of establishing control in the north.

The general air of paranoia and discontent in the north gave way to the Holy Spirit Movement, led by Alice Auma Lakwena, who offered her followers protection from Museveni's soldiers, and promised Acholis a spiritual cleansing and redemption from all the violence that had both been done to them and been done by their bitter, haunted soldiers. Such salvation required them to, among other things, rub shea butter on themselves to evade bullets. Lakwena claimed that snakes, bees, and rivers would devour their enemies. Before the army defeated Lakwena and her legions of footmen, thousands of supporters and innocent civilians had died during battle.

Joseph Kony was her cousin. A former altar boy who dropped out of school, he was regarded by his community as a healer, able to lift curses and cure illnesses. He started the LRA in his twenties, when he said the Holy Spirit had visited him and told him to overthrow the government. He claimed the army was going to murder everyone in Acholiland. He vowed to recover the land and cattle stolen from the Acholis. The late 1980s was a time when resistance efforts against the government had genuine popular support among northerners. Kony recruited a contingent of Acholi ex-soldiers who called themselves the Black Battalion. But Acholis soon realized how sadistic the LRA was: Kony declared that the country should be ruled by the Ten Commandments; that it was now his duty to perform a cleansing on Acholiland and root out all evil in the world; and that he was possessed by spirits and powers, a claim that led many of his terrified followers to consider him a Godlike being.

When many Acholis refused to support his delusions, Kony turned on his own people. In the early 1990s, the LRA began attacking the very population it was claiming to protect. By the decade's end, the group was composed almost entirely of members who had been kidnapped against their will, usually children. The longer children spent in the group, the more brutal they often became and the farther up the ranks they rose. Brainwashed and desensitized to violence, they eventually became commanders.

President Museveni was equally culpable for the trauma and poverty that plagued the region. A period of relative stability and prosperity arrived after he took office, but the wealth didn't spread north of the Nile River. Some suspected that Museveni's government was even enriching itself off the war, by inflating its military budget as it took money from foreign donors and prolonged the fighting. The government's counterinsurgency sent many Acholis, mostly subsistence farmers, into displacement camps in order to empty rural villages of recruits and support for the LRA. People were forced to leave their green land. In the camps, many became infected with diseases because of cramped conditions and poor sanitation. People fell hungry, fell into despair, fell victim to violence, and were still, incredibly, abducted under the noses of the soldiers tasked to guard them. The army was also burning the homes of northerners and slashing their crops, executing LRA suspects, beating people and accusing them of collaborating with the rebels. "They are your children," the soldiers told them.

For over a quarter of a century, the LRA carried out an unprecedented reign of terror, first in northern Uganda, and then in neighboring South Sudan, the Democratic Republic of the Congo, and the Central African Republic. The killing, mutilating, abducting, and looting had become completely divorced from Kony's stated revolutionary political goal—restoring Acholi dominance. In a warped reading of the Bible, Kony instructed rebels to cut off the lips, ears, and noses of their victims, to amputate their arms and legs if they rode bicycles on the Sabbath, and any other kind of medieval punishment imaginable. The LRA forcibly recruited some 30,000 children from northern Uganda into its ranks and displaced 2 million people in the region. A 2006 cease-fire between the rebels and the Ugandan government was intended to finally end the LRA's operations in the north.

The town of Gulu was the epicenter of the LRA's uprising. Its chairman, or local leader, the bright and energetic Martin Mapenduzi, met Kony twice during peace talks in South Sudan. Once was in the dense jungle of the Garamba National Park in the Democratic Republic of the Congo, where Kony spoke for two hours straight. Some northern members of Mapenduzi's government-appointed negotiation team were almost persuaded by Kony's accusations against Museveni of corruption, bias in employment and military recruitment, and economic neglect. Kony struck Mapenduzi as unpredictable and paranoid, though clever. His team told the warlord that people were ready to forgive him. But LRA leaders bristled when Mapenduzi explained that there would have to be some accountability for their crimes, and that International Criminal Court indictments against Kony and his deputies still stood. Various clergy appealed to Kony, to no avail. So as Kony negotiated a peace agreement, he was secretly moving fighters to the Central African Republic. In the spring of 2008, at the final signing ceremony of the peace agreement, he simply never showed up.

After taking advantage of the Central African Republic's heavily forested and weakly governed areas already rife with bandits, Kony was believed to be hiding in Sudan. His foot soldiers were still kidnapping and killing through the region. In 2011, the United States tried to capture or kill Kony by sending one hundred special forces to Uganda, South Sudan, the Congo, and the Central African Republic to help the African Union force, made up primarily of Ugandan troops, hunt the rebels. But the Ugandans complained of insufficient equipment, lack of intelligence on the rebels' whereabouts, and meager food rations. The nonprofit Invisible Children released a viral video on the warlord in 2012; Kony still proved elusive. In 2014, the United States sent more military aircraft and special forces to help. A few key LRA leaders had surrendered or been captured or killed. But the LRA's independence from technology was one of their greatest assets, allowing them to avoid their hunters by using messengers and handwritten letters to communicate, and eschewing phones and two-way radios. U.S. officials acknowledged the rebels were unlike any other enemy they had faced. And in early 2017, the Americans and the Ugandans announced they would be withdrawing their missions from the Central African Republic.

Even though the LRA was no longer in Uganda, its ghosts hovered in the uneasy peace. Families across Uganda had not only members who had been killed, raped, and disfigured by rebels, but also those who were forced into the LRA and had now returned. Until May 2012, LRA combatants who either surrendered or escaped were granted amnesty by the Ugandan government. Over 13,000 fighters received amnesty, and many were given the option to join the army. They now slept next to soldiers, their former enemies, in Ugandan military garrisons as they hunted for their old comrades. Other ex-fighters, and sex slaves and porters, settled near people they may have once harmed, and their former communities didn't know what to do with them. Nearly all were kidnapped as children, but their actions after the abductions were usually appalling. Children were forced to kill their parents and then, sometimes, eat a meal with their hands still soaked in blood. Communities were struggling in the aftermath.

Now a scraggly group of a few hundred members, the LRA was rapidly losing fighters. High-ranking rebels who had long wanted to escape were sending home their "bush wives" and children, armed with letters instructing the men's families to take the women and children in and take care of them. When, and if, the men escaped themselves, the young mothers were agreeing to marry them with a surprising frequency, confounding families who were left gasping for breath, trying to steady their vision, when their daughters were first taken.

Eunice grew up in a village seven miles outside Gulu, a town with roads extending like arteries into the countryside. The paths out of Gulu weaved past uniformed children walking to school, men and women riding bicycles as they lugged farm tools and jerry cans of water, and sun-drenched bursts of color, from the lime-toned bushes and banana trees to the rust-colored earth. Mango and orange trees surrounded the spread-out homes of Eunice's family and her neighbors. It was in this serene landscape where Eunice jumped rope with her sisters and eagerly learned to cook from her mother. She liked to perform the dances traditional to Acholiland, and went on adventures with her best friend in the nearby creeks and bushes. Eunice was quiet in class but liked school, and she felt hurt when she had to stop attending in the fifth grade. Her father had stopped supporting her mother, and he no longer paid Eunice's school fees. He had other women who took up his time and his money, and Eunice watched helplessly as her mother struggled to brew and sell a local, potent alcohol to make an income. She soon joined the business, helping brew alcohol and sewing tablecloths. But despite feeling abandoned, she loved her father. When he died from heart disease when Eunice was twelve, the blow felt worse than anything she had ever experienced.

One day soon after her father's death, her relatives heard that the LRA was attacking nearby villages. Many of the children and adults in her extended family decided to sleep in the bushes for a few nights, hiding amid the foliage. Villagers considered it safer to sleep in the forest to avoid the rebels if they showed up on a surprise raid. Eunice heard gunshots that second night. When she returned home early in the morning, she found her brother, sister-in-law, and cousin dead. Everything else was ash. The rebels had burned down their houses and belongings. It was now daylight, and the rebels had done what they came to do, so Eunice knew they were no longer around. But she felt their presence and couldn't stop shivering. The horrific experience seemed to bring the family together. Despite the complications of her father having had so many partners, the women and their children got along well, and Eunice was close with both her full and half sisters.

By the time Eunice turned fifteen, in 1996, life had settled into a surreal kind of normal despite the chaos the LRA was wreaking around her community. The rebels had taken and killed relatives of hers. She slept in the bushes if the LRA was operating close to home, or traveled to Gulu to spend the night in a shelter like thousands of other "night commuters," children who poured into the town from the vulnerable countryside to sleep. But she refused to restrict her life by the persistent threat of the rebels. She was planning on making her third trip to visit her older sister Doreen at St. Mary's College, a boarding school in Apac, just south of Gulu.

It was a great source of pride for the family to have Doreen in the school. "I was so excited to see her," Eunice recalled. She expected to eventually go back to school herself. She packed a bag of bread, cooking oil, and sweet treats to bring her sister, and boarded a *matatu*, or minibus, for the journey. The first night after she arrived, in October, was filled with gossip and laughter with Doreen and her sister's friends, poised young women who made Eunice feel both full of admiration and at ease. The second night, there had been food, soda, and dancing as the girls celebrated Uganda's Independence Day. Then, in the black early hours of the morning, the rebels came and took her, her sister, and all of her new friends from their beds. Eunice had been sleeping when strange men wielding flashlights woke her up. They were shouting at the girls to get up and open the door of their dorm. There was the sound of breaking glass from the windows. Girls tried to hide under their bunk beds as the rebels forced themselves into the room. They were mostly teenage boys with guns, wild and unkempt, banging on their beds' headboards and dragging girls out from under the beds and into the cold night. The girls were screaming. Some fought back and the rebels hit them, a few others managed to run away. Ribbons still adorned their bedposts.

Outside of the dormitories, men, and some women, were everywhere, 200 of them or more. There was nowhere to run. They forced the girls into lines, and she and Doreen were tied together with rope in the same formation and ordered to walk barefoot, rebels with flashlights leading the way. The journey through forest and fields of elephant grass was arduous: Their feet stung and the rope choked their waists whenever a girl fell. Along the way, things seemed to move at double speed. The rebels told them little. Occasionally they untied the schoolgirls, forcing them to cook and clean during hurried rest stops in the bush. The girls watched as the rebels kidnapped other people they encountered along the way, adding to their group of captives. They hid when the rebels clashed with bands of government soldiers. During skirmishes, the rebels clustered the girls together for protection under mango trees as bullets crashed around them. When army helicopters flew overhead, they held broad cassava leaves over their heads as they moved to escape detection. At those times, Eunice and Doreen would find each other. "I used to ask my sister, 'What can we do? Can we escape?' But my sister told me to keep quiet, that if they heard me, they would kill me," Eunice recalled. She worried about her mother and other relatives at home, and had nightmares of what would come next.

A geography teacher at St. Mary's College, John Bosco, and the deputy headmistress, an Italian nun named Sister Rachele Fassera, had followed the girls into the bush by tracing the wrappers of candy the rebels had looted from the school. Upon reaching them, they confronted the rebels, pleading with them to release their students. The rebel in command, Marianno Ochaya Lagira, initially agreed to release the girls. He then changed his mind and said he would only free 109 of the 139 girls. The girls begged the nun: If they had to stay, they knew they would be raped. Most had never touched a boy intimately. They knew they would never see their families again. They knew they would be ruined.

As the rebels divided the girls into two groups, one girl tried to slip into the group going home, but Sister Rachele told her to go back; she was jeopardizing the lives of the others. Eunice watched the negotiations with cautious hope and then foreboding. Sometimes she couldn't tell if she was dreaming or awake. What would happen to her? In the end, the rebels let 109 girls go home. Doreen could leave. Eunice had to stay. She was stunned. The departing girls who had brought sweaters gave them to the girls who were left behind. Then they left in a long line through the bush.

For several days, the rebels made Eunice and the other girls trudge through the bush and even fight each other. On a Friday, they came across a woman farming. One of the rebels told the woman that she needed to be punished because Kony had issued an edict that forbade work on Fridays. He told Eunice to cut the woman's hand off with a machete. "I felt so bad. But they told me if I didn't do it, they would kill me," she said. "So I found the strength to do it because I didn't want to die."

Bosco had much in common with Eunice. His mother, Auma, raised him and his seven brothers and sisters alone in another village outside Gulu, just five or so miles from Eunice's. Their modest hut sat on land long owned by his extended family; the compound of homes was covered in beans, cassava, corn, dense banana trees, and mango trees with leaves that fanned out against the sky. Bosco's father had married twice and had often left him, his mother, and his siblings to fend for themselves in favor of his second wife and their children. He rarely visited. "He pretended that he loved us, but he didn't really that much," Bosco recalled. But he was happy. "Life was easy because we farmed and had enough food; it was only a challenge to get enough money to go to school," he said. Money was tight, but his mother would take them to Gulu once a year to shop for clothes for holidays and special occasions. A lanky kid with watchful eyes and a radiant smile, he loved playing soccer with his brothers and friends, and liked his math and religion classes the most. Bosco was stubborn and loud in class, and popular, but he enjoyed helping his mother on the weekends with the farming, digging and planting crops.

At night, Bosco slept alongside his brothers and sisters in the hut's main room: a tangle of limbs on the papyrus mats they laid on the ground. The children played and fought, especially when one tried to sneak off with another's prized possessions, but they tried to look out for each other. "The days went quickly," Bosco recalled. When they woke up, they washed their faces, swept the compound, and then went to school or helped with the farming. His best friend was his attentive younger brother Robin. Small and skinny, Robin was a skilled bird-hunting partner. "He was a boy who liked people and really listened to them," Bosco said.

His mother tried to hide her worries from her children. But at around the age of ten, Bosco began hearing talk of the rebels. The LRA was taking children to Sudan, where they couldn't escape. After a few years, his mother told Bosco that she wanted him and his two younger brothers to start sleeping in the bush every night to prevent being kidnapped. The LRA's insurgency was intensifying, and they had attacked nearby villages. Students and teachers had stopped going to schools. "I believed God would protect me from the LRA," Bosco said. "There was nothing we could do: We could not go to Gulu because we did not have land there, so we lived in the bush."

Bosco and his siblings encountered their neighbors in the forest, other children who had been sent there for protection. There were about ten of them hiding together. Their parents and grandparents stayed at home and cooked meals for the children in the bush, bringing them at regular intervals. Bosco and the others weaved simple mats together from the wide leaves of coconut trees. They bathed in a stream and collected water to drink in plastic jugs. They weren't far from their homes, but might as well have been thousands of miles away. None of them were accustomed to this way of life. Their bodies itched from the grass, branches, and rocks poking at them. Many got scabies. Some came down with malaria from the hordes of mosquitoes. The boys and girls took turns climbing trees to look out for rebels. "We were always scared. You didn't want them to see you looking out," Bosco recalled.

Often, when people in his village heard that the LRA was operating elsewhere, Bosco would return home during the day. He had gone back to the village one afternoon and was helping his mother tend to the crops in the field, when they heard a gunshot. His mother ran toward the giant mango tree on their compound where they thought the sound had come from. When she reached it, she cried out, warning Bosco not to join her. Robin was dead. The LRA had entered the compound and had come across him sitting under the tree; when Robin tried to run away, the rebels shot him. Bosco was devastated.

Bosco's days became grim. He had stopped going to school, as his friends and cousins were taken. "I was so worried that at any time, any day, the rebels could come for me," he said. He had been sleeping in the bush for two years and was tired. One night, the air was cold and starting to release fat drops of rain. At around two in the morning, he and his brothers and cousins snuck back into his hut and curled into the floor to sleep. It took only two hours for the rebels to arrive. One pushed in the door and trained a flashlight on Bosco's face for what seemed like several minutes. He asked if Bosco was a soldier; Bosco told him he was not, and the rebel began kicking him. Another man was beating his mother, who cried for her sons. Rebels filled the compound and told the children that they were at a good age to be trained. They gave Bosco a heavy, loaded gun to carry, and took forty children from his village and neighboring ones that night. They left his mother at home, helpless and full of fear.

After hours of walking, the rebels ordered the children to sit down in a circle and told them there was no hope of escaping. They pushed Bosco's brother Patrick into the middle of the circle and made him sit down. A man then took a machete and cut a cross into Patrick's head and chest, killing him. He then cut off Patrick's hand and put it inside the boy's open stomach. Bosco felt numb. Badly beaten and in shock, he was sure that he would be killed next. To scare the children from running, the rebels forced each child to take the hand out of Patrick's stomach and then put it back inside. Four children refused and were executed. Bosco removed the hand and put it back inside.

As the group trekked to an LRA base in southern Sudan, Bosco watched as his schoolmates were killed when their feet became too swollen to walk. "I had to learn to take care of myself," he said. Oddly enough, despite the brutality, life with the LRA was initially better than his life in hiding. Bosco was sleeping out in the open again without a mosquito net, this time on a plastic tarp the rebels had stolen while raiding villages. When he had been hiding, Bosco was afraid to snore or even breathe loudly so that he would not be heard. With the rebels, he could at least sleep more soundly because they had already found him. There was no point in sleeping in a tent since there was never enough time to collect all their supplies and run. The rebels were always on the move in Uganda, evading and fighting the military. In southern Sudan, they had a base where they could rest. The Sudanese government was providing material support like food, land for their camps, and guns to the LRA, in retaliation for the Ugandan government supporting southern Sudanese rebels. It also expected the LRA to attack those rebels fighting the Sudanese government, the Sudan People's Liberation Army, which the Ugandan militants did.

But Bosco was angry and did things that weren't good. "I wanted to kill all the government soldiers. I was confused and didn't know what was happening," he said. He did not trust the military. Soldiers had burned the homes of people he knew, sometimes killing them, and then blamed the rebels for the crimes. He was furious with both the military, for hurting his people, and with the LRA, for doing the same. The LRA encouraged him to think of the government as the enemy.

The rebels immediately put Bosco and the rest of the children to work by sending them back into the villages where they grew up to abduct and kill people. Their goal was to turn the children into monsters who believed that even if they escaped, their communities would not accept them back. Bosco and the kids who had survived thus far were so scared of dying that they would have done anything to save themselves. That was how they had survived so long, after all, unlike the boys and girls they had watched the rebels kill after they refused to beat innocent people or each other. But it was a sick twist of fate to be forced to inflict the same cruelty that he had suffered. "When I came upon children, I wanted to shout to them that I was a rebel and that they better run away, but I was never alone and able to do so," he said. "I didn't want to kill people, but I was more afraid of being killed."

He mostly wore T-shirts and slacks, though on some raids he would wear the green standard-issue trousers and shirt Ugandan soldiers wore; the rebels stole them off their dead bodies. He was chosen to be a bodyguard for a commander. Bosco was "active and really sharp," he said, and could do things quickly, like gathering bullets and guns after a gunfight and running to help the wounded or vulnerable. He followed Kony's order to never flinch in battle, to run into the fighting first with the other children, and to show no emotion. At night, even in Sudan, he remained outside to guard his commander's tent, lying down on the prickly ground and trying to make it bearable. When it rained, violent gushes of water came down on him for hours on end. Sometimes he would have to hold his face up to the downpour for several minutes, letting the rain wash over him. Kony had told them the water was sacred.

He and the rebels rarely spent more than one night in the same place. The walking was punishing, under a bare, heavy sun, over steep hills, often with little water and food. Children were beaten or killed if they fell behind. Those who collapsed of exhaustion or illness, or who fell into the rivers they crossed, were left to die. They roamed in groups of around 200 fighters, with porters and sex slaves. At the group's peak, in the late 1990s, there were about 3,000 fighters.

When the rebels reached a place where they wanted to build camp, they flattened the grass and chopped down the smaller trees to create a clearing. They slept on blankets looted from villages; mattresses went to the commanders. After setting up camp, the commanders of each group would sleep at a center point, with several groups of fighters sleeping around them in rings that stretched outward for miles to protect the center. Kony was at the absolute nucleus. The newly abducted slept near the commanders to prevent escapes—if they ran away, they would stumble upon the other fighters stationed farther away. The effect was a vast spiderweb.

Life took on a perverse new routine. When Bosco woke up in the morning, he began his assigned duty. Some of the boys had to loot food, others climb trees and spy, and still others patrol the perimeters of the camp. They worked a five-to-six-hour shift; ate a meal, which was often cooked wild leaves and beans, or goat and chicken if they were lucky; and then worked another shift. There was no doctor. People around him died of cholera and other diseases they couldn't treat without medicine.

By the time he met Eunice, three years later, Bosco thought he had lost everything and everyone he had once loved. He refused to think about his family, and had started to regard some of his fellow soldiers as friends. In a way, he saw Eunice as one of his old playmates who would help him erase the painful past and figure out how to live in the present. "With Eunice, I believed that we could begin a new family," he said. "She was the first person in the bush I wanted to love."

The commanders, after they had taken their girls, told him to select the one he liked. He was excited. Even much later, he would refer not to meeting Eunice but to "getting" her, like a gift.

Eunice's first night with Bosco at the camp felt like another nightmare. He asked her to sleep with him, and she refused. He insisted, and raped her—her first sexual experience. The following months were strained and uncomfortable. Eunice was depressed and afraid of him. At night, she listened to the sound of birds crying while lying on her mat woven of grass, leaves, and branches, and longing for home. After the other girls had gone back home with the Italian nun, the remaining schoolgirls marched to Sudan.

The new country was a lonely, desolate landscape. They had endured weeks of the girls being forced to hurt and kill villagers, doing things like smashing in the heads of other abducted children. One girl, not from the school, tried to escape, and the rebels forced some of the schoolgirls to beat her to death with tree logs. The girls were beaten themselves by the rebels for any reason, including expressing pain. They had to wake up before sunrise and walk until sunset, with only a break for lunch. It felt like the army was always just a few steps behind them, ready to throw a rocket grenade at Eunice at any moment. The rebels anointed the girls with shea oil, for protection, but Eunice knew it was a sham.

Her moments with Bosco were brief. Bosco slept mostly outside of their tent, like the other men, to guard it. He was sent on raids that took him away from their group for days at a time. Eunice tried to escape once but was caught. She and her friend, a young woman like herself, had been washing clothes in a stream when they decided to run. Rebels stationed high in the trees working as lookouts spotted them. Bosco had defended her, prevented her from being killed.

Every day, if there was not a battle, she woke up, collected water, washed the clothes, cooked, and then sat and talked with her sister's friends, now wives to other rebels, before going to sleep. On his forays away from camp, Bosco wanted to be back with Eunice, but he sensed her fear around him and set about trying to win her trust. When LRA leaders asked Eunice to participate on looting or abduction trips, Bosco would lie to them and say that he had ordered her to perform other tasks. She still occasionally had to go on those raids, and so he shielded her in battle. During food shortages in the camp, he scrounged up water and bread and brought it to their tent to surprise her. Those periods of hunger were excruciating; they had to dig up wild cassava, roots, and leaves to quell their empty stomachs. For Bosco, life had improved immensely. The pair cooked together, made a home, and worked together to move their belongings when they shifted locations—it was what he had long wanted.

Eunice noticed his devotion. "I would tell him my fears and he would encourage me. I started feeling free with him because I thought he was the only one who could help me," Eunice said of their first years. "We were happy to have each other because we thought we were all we had left. It was not easy to return home, so we got used to the life. We chatted, we laughed." She became resigned to her fate, and felt that it was time to be practical. She watched Bosco and saw a boy who had been forceful and insensitive, but who seemed to care about her and was also resigned to his own fate. As the years passed, she stopped hiding her feelings. She realized that she respected him.

Four years after their first meeting, Eunice, now nineteen, had their first child, a boy they named Edimon. Bosco was twenty-three. It was the happiest day for each since before their abductions. They each spent as much time as they could with their son, and caring for him brought them together. They confided in each other about their pasts and families. "I felt like he was the closest person to me on Earth. Especially after I became pregnant, he started taking me in closer to him and asking how we could make our future together," Eunice remembered. The commanders sometimes played the radio after acquiring a successful bounty of captives and food, and songs from their childhood would float into their tent. "We used to hear the music, and it would feel so good, though it would make me think of home," she said.

Kony reassured his group that they would rule Uganda

one day, and the couple imagined what life would be like once Bosco was a rich government minister. During battle, Bosco took notice of how fat the government soldiers were; someday, he knew he would be equally as well fed. In the late 1990s, the group had several thousand members, and it wasn't a stretch to believe they could be victorious. At their base in Sudan, they had solar panels and radio transmitters provided by the Sudanese government. It was only years later, when gunfight after gunfight had produced little change in their circumstances, did he begin to see Kony was lying to them. There would be no redemption for the LRA's child soldiers.

Eunice told the other women that Bosco was kind, but that he had a temper. As the women, including a few of the girls with whom she was kidnapped, gathered firewood in the mornings, they furtively compared notes on their lives and gave each other advice and encouragement. They would also talk about going home. Three years after their son's birth, Eunice gathered the courage to tell Bosco that she was still thinking about what it would be like to go home. He confessed that he had been thinking about it, too. A radio station in Gulu called 102 Mega FM had launched a show broadcasting messages from rebels who had escaped or surrendered, and who announced that it was safe to come home. LRA commanders would angrily turn off the radio when the show came on a couple of evenings a week, and say that the messages had been recorded before the army executed the returned rebels. LRA leaders liked to listen to the radio to keep updated on world news. Bosco had begun to have doubts, however. Eunice was pregnant again, and she struggled to carry their son, a gun, and their belongings during battle. She hated the reality that they could be ambushed at any moment. They knew that the bush was not a place to raise a family.

Bosco had tried to escape twice himself. When he was caught, he lied and said he had seen people walking near the camp and tried to capture them, but they had run away too quickly. A few of the rebels did not believe him and said he should be killed. But he was spared. That instance was before he had met Eunice. The second time was part of a plan they devised together. "I told her she should first escape, then I would follow her a few days later," Bosco said. Before they could carry out the plan, though, their commanders split their group into two smaller units. The two were separated. When their groups reunited, he didn't see Eunice. He assumed she and their son had gotten away, so he tried as well. When he was caught leaving the camp, he saw her. She had been placed into yet another group. The couple vowed to try again.

One morning almost a year later, while gathering firewood, with their baby on her back, food strapped to her stomach, and water in a jerry can balanced on her head, Eunice simply walked away from the camp and didn't stop walking until night fell. Bosco planned to wait to hear Eunice's message on 102 Mega FM, and then, when he was assured that she and their son were alive, he would try to join them. He had seen other men let their wives escape. Sometimes the men were blamed and killed; other times they successfully claimed that they had lost their wives in battle. He planned to say the same thing. "The plan was that Eunice would escape and then go to a rehabilitation center, and then our children would go to school," Bosco said. The morning she escaped, Eunice was afraid and wanted them to leave together. Bosco told her it was too risky. He held Eunice and their son. He then repeated the name of his home village and wished them well. After she left, he guarded the route she took into the forest. He was almost too anxious and scared to breathe. "If they had found out I had freed her, the others would have followed her and killed her," Bosco said.

He went back to camp and waited.

2

MAURITANIA

Not Restrained by Chains

HABY MINT RABAH was born in 1974 in the sand-swept outpost of Mederdra, in southwestern Mauritania. She was her parents' oldest child, frail in build but tough and smart. Her parents were slaves for different masters, nomadic families who belonged to the same clan. The families occasionally converged on the same grazing land with their animals, and her parents met that way, eventually having two daughters and two sons. They were not allowed to marry. Haby's mother, Selmana, left her when she was an infant in the care of Haby's grandmother, Barakettou, who worked for yet another family in the clan. Slaves in Mauritania are forced to work as domestic servants, camel and goat herders, and other menial jobs from early childhood, and in the same families that their mothers and grandmothers also worked.

When Haby thought of her grandmother, she remembered her very dark skin, and her kindness. Memories of her brief time in Barakettou's care were vague but warm: playing with the other young children, feeling fed and safe. The slave-owning families lived in a cluster of spacious and comfortable tents. Their slaves usually slept and ate in the same quarters as the animals. Haby was mostly sheltered from the work her grandmother did. But one day when Haby was eight, Barakettou's masters woke her up and informed her that her grandmother had passed away. They told her to get help from the other slaves to bury the body. Haby came to think of her grandmother's burial site, in a lonesome corner of the desert, as the place where her childhood ended.

Things began to happen very quickly after Haby's grandmother died. Barakettou's former masters took Haby's mother, Selmana, as their slave; Haby's siblings had already been sent to other families in the clan. Selmana's former masters, an adult brother and sister named Abdoulaye and Aminetou, now took in Haby to be their slave. "I took care of the animals from early morning until night, every day," Haby recalled. "I took care of all of their needs, and after tending to the animals, I had to fetch water and cook for my masters. I did this work every day, regardless if it was hot or cold, they didn't care." If Haby was too tired and didn't wake up around dawn, Abdoulaye would come and wake her, shouting insults at her. She was not human, her master told her. There was no time for washing up or eating. Haby went straight to feed the goats, sheep, and donkeys, and then led them under the blazing sun in search of grazing field. "I spent the whole day walking with them," Haby said. She carried only a stick to keep them in line, and a single bottle of water.

If Haby returned late from drawing water at the well, her masters shouted at her. Abdoulaye beat her, especially if Aminetou told him that Haby did not do her tasks exactly like how she had wanted them. "He hit me, called me a slave," Haby said. "He would come to me and beat me, saying that my body needed to be beaten to be put in shape. He said I have to be beaten from time to time, because if I am not beaten, I will forget that someone is over me. I spent my life like this." For meals, Haby cooked the siblings rice with a peanut sauce, and meat if there was any. They always complained about her cooking. Nothing she did was good enough. They hit her constantly. The worst of Haby's jobs was gathering firewood. When she went into the bush, Abdoulaye often followed to rape her. Haby was raped on so many occasions that she lost count.

"Sometimes I would be so tired I didn't even have the energy to eat, or to eat only just a bit," Haby recalled. "When I finished cooking, I then took food to the animals." After midnight, she could finally collapse on a piece of plastic.

Haby never laughed. She had no friends, no time for leisure, and nothing to call her own. She wasn't even allowed to cover her hair, to have any kind of modesty. She spent much of her time alone, or with her masters. She watched children go to the Islamic schools nearby with jealousy. She couldn't read the Koran. She had to ask permission from her masters to pray, and was told her soul was not worthy of prayer. "I didn't even know how to pray, how to practice my religion," she said.

Haby's master, Aminetou, was divorced and childless, and Aminetou's brother had married twice and had four children. When the women and children visited, Haby also served them. As the family slept in their tents, she had to sleep in the open air under a veil and tree branches, a flimsy shield against the world.

In 1981, Mauritania's government abolished slavery, becoming the last country in the world to do so. But the presidential decree offered no legal provision to punish slave owners. In 2007, under international pressure, the government passed a law that allowed slaveholders to be prosecuted. Yet slavery persisted, even as the government and religious leaders denied it. In 2013, the Global Slavery Index estimated that at least 140,000 people were enslaved in Mauritania, out of a population of 3.8 million.

Women and children make up most of Mauritania's slave class. When boys come of age, they sometimes manage to leave their masters' families. Adult women are considered minors by Mauritanian custom, and female slaves face greater difficulty escaping. In the countryside, entire communities of slaves live in the service of their masters, on call for labor whenever they are needed.

Whenever Haby lay down, she felt a sharp ache, somewhere deep, that hurt when she tried to fall asleep. She thought of her brothers and sister, and her mother—

would she spend time with them again? She was in her twenties now; it had been so long. Everyone had always told her she looked just like her mother, Selmana, with her small-boned face, burnished tan skin, and serene way of taking up as little space as possible, but Haby barely knew her at all. There was no time to be together. When the various families in the clan set up camp near each other, Selmana would come and spend the night with Haby, but such occasions were rare. Haby was "following her elders," the older slaves of the other masters, and copying their example. They were doing the same work she was doing. "When I saw the elder slaves working, I remembered my mother and the way she was suffering," she said. But how could she wish for something different? This was her life.

Her brother Bilal visited her twice in those years. Bilal had left his masters at nineteen after they beat him so badly he finally ran away. When she took the animals out for grazing and water during his visits, Bilal accompanied her and tried to persuade her to leave with him. Haby had often dreamed of leaving her masters. She had tried to run away twice. Abdoulaye followed her both times, brought her back, and hit her until she was bleeding and broken. Her masters intimidated her, threatening to send the police after her if she tried fleeing again. Haby told her brother to leave her alone. Escape was not possible for her. Their own mother had told her to stay. "I felt horrible, that it wasn't right for my mother to tell me to obey my masters, but I did not want to argue with her," Haby said. Her masters claimed that another kind of life would be unbearable. "Even though they beat me, even though they were against me, they were all I knew," she said.

Haby's life was not without love. Selmana always told her that she loved her, and Haby believed it. But by the time Haby was in her early thirties, her mother had died—she had not even known Selmana was sick—and Haby had conceived two children from the rapes. They were both sweet boys: Yessar, who was born disabled, and Mohamed. She only knew the year Mohamed was born, 2006, because it was the same year Saddam Hussein was executed; otherwise the years passed without significance.

Like other children of slaves, Yessar and Mohamed were also considered slaves. But in 2008, Haby began hearing on the radio that activists were bringing court cases against slave owners. Her masters became nervous. They told Haby she was free, but they also told her the activists were criminals working for the United States and Israel. "It was a way to keep me with them," Haby said. If anyone asked her about her situation, her masters warned her, she should say that she was not a slave.

Within a few months, Bilal sent a woman bearing a message to where Haby was staying with her masters in Mederdra. Haby didn't know the woman, but the message was clear: Bilal was coming to take her away from this place. One afternoon in 2008, a relative of her masters was visiting, and Abdoulaye told her to go braid the hair of one of the relative's slaves. Haby was with the girl in a tent when she heard a commotion. She picked up Mohamed and rushed outside; she saw Bilal, a policeman, an unfamiliar woman, and a man she had heard about on the radio, an activist named Biram.

"Come with us," Biram, a dark, lean man who was strangely confident, said to her.

Haby panicked. "I'm not going!" she screamed. Her master had said that the police would punish her if she tried to escape. A policeman was there now. Was it all a trick? Bilal approached her and shouted that she must come with them.

"Let's go!" Biram yelled.

"So do you want to leave or not?" the policeman asked her.

"You're leaving, you're leaving. Stay silent. You're leaving," Bilal said.

"I am not a slave, and I'm not leaving with them," Haby said, raising her hand angrily.

"Hear me well, these people say that you're a slave," the policeman said. "If you are a slave, you have to leave."

"I am not a slave! I am not a slave! I am free! I am a slave of God!" she said. "Officer, see my brother? I disown him, I'm not leaving with him."

"But you are a slave!" Bilal erupted.

It was chaos, voices crashing into each other, shouting and arguing, and Haby couldn't think. She held Mohamed close, told the men not to touch her. Her black veil rippled in the wind. "I'm not moving, I'm not moving," she said.

With the policeman in tow, Biram and Bilal took Haby to their black pickup truck and put her inside. Aminetou, in a green veil, followed them. "Hey you, stay away from the car," Biram told her. "Bid her farewell and disappear." Haby, who was now thirty-four, denied that Aminetou was her master. Biram shouted at the siblings that justice would catch up to them. He told Haby to stay in the car. She insulted Biram, shoving him away from her. Biram grabbed Yessar from the tent and then placed him on Haby's lap. On the drive to Mauritania's capital city, Nouakchott, about sixty miles north, Haby was in shock. She wondered if Biram was going to kill her. She began crying hysterically. "I really hated him," Haby said. She believed he was a traitor.

Biram and Bilal took Haby to Biram's house, where she kept to herself, uneasily waiting for her masters to find her. After a few days in the safety of Biram's house, Haby began to relax. She could sleep as much as she wanted; she had food to eat; there was no work for her to do. Biram, she learned, worked with a group of activists, men and women who had gone to school and prayed as well as her masters did, to free slaves around the country. They were starting to teach her how to read and pray, and she joined a sewing instruction project they ran for women who were once enslaved. Haby embarked on a new path. She made friends and married quickly; it ended in divorce. A second marriage left her a widow, and her son, Yessar, passed away. But Haby was so dazed by freedom that she rushed headfirst into life, enjoying her right to make her own money, marry whoever and whenever she wanted, be her own master. Liberty had at first left her disoriented, unsure if she could be on her own, and then it opened her up. Haby offered the activists her help. She later met and married her current husband, Hassan, a soldier with whom life had become stable and simple. "Life with him is good, inshallah," Haby said.

When I first met her in 2014, Haby was forty, still delicate-looking in pastel-shaded hijabs. I visited her again the next year, and she calmly sat on the floor of an activist's living room, where she pulled her legs in close and folded her body over itself. She was quietly observant, but at times unabashedly outspoken—she kept teasing the activists, asking what important tasks took up so much of their time that they didn't visit her anymore, making them laugh. She called Biram a hero for freeing her and helping her afterward, but seemed to understand that it required her own reserve of strength to make it out alive. "I became a human being. My child goes to school," she told me. She took care of him, and of the home they shared with Hassan, and she worked selling vegetables and tea at a modest stand. The first time we talked, her son Mohamed was in another room watching television. Haby began crying. She was happy, she said, but full of regret for the people she knew who were still enslaved. "As long as there is slavery in Mauritania, I will always feel that I am not fully free."

Over the course of centuries, Berbers from North Africa and Arabs came to inhabit what is now Mauritania. They took black African slaves, creating an entrenched racial hierarchy. Over time, the bloodlines of the masters and the slaves mixed and they came to share a language—Arabic or an Arabic dialect—and cultural practices: As the masters imposed their traditions, the slaves lost their own.

As a result, and disturbingly, slave owners often referred to their slaves as family. In modern Mauritania, people speak of the mingled Arab–Berbers as White Moors and the slaves as Haratin. White Moors, a minority, hold most of the country's wealth and political power. Haratin, who have dark skin, are a permanent underclass, even after they are freed. Haby and Biram, the activist who freed her, were Haratin. Somewhere between these two castes are Afro-Mauritanians, ethnic groups also found in Senegal that have never been enslaved. People endured slavelike conditions in nearby countries, but slavery in Mauritania was unusually severe and persistent. Because of those extreme conditions, the antislavery movement in Mauritania had become among the most radical activist movements in Africa.

With around 4 million people, Mauritania stands at the crossroads of sub-Saharan and northern Africa, a vast desert landscape that reaches to where the Atlantic Ocean consumes the coastline in West Africa. Along the way, sand dunes swirl down to iron-ore pits in the Sahara. It has long been a poor place, supported mostly by mining and fishing, and by military aid from the West, given in exchange for the Mauritanian government's help in fighting terrorism in the region. Ever since a drought struck the strip of desert and savanna on the southern edge of the Sahara called the Sahel in the 1960s, the country has been collapsing in on its cities, as nomads and farmers in search of work migrate from sandy hinterlands to slightly less sandy urban areas.

The emptiness of Mauritania was a blessing and a curse

to its darkest-skinned inhabitants. In all that space, there was room to grow unhindered, spread out your family, and claim territory if you were lucky. You could be left alone, almost disappear in the mounds of sand and prickly shrubbery. You could also be ignored and neglected, praying to be noticed as you endure the unspeakable. For anyone who was enslaved in that country, the emptiness was the only neutral witness to their suffering. There was no one looking or listening, at least not anyone who cared. It would take time before they became used to the noise of the activists who came to free them.

I arrived in the Mauritanian capital, Nouakchott, in late January 2014 from my home base in Lagos, Nigeria. I wanted to see the place where, almost unbelievably, widespread slavery still existed, and to meet the man who was fighting back. It took two flights: one to Senegal, which lies just under Mauritania, and its seaside capital city, Dakar, where I stayed for a night with a photographer friend in her apartment that faced the sea. After a quick pancake breakfast the next morning, I boarded a Senegal Air flight to Nouakchott.

I was a little uneasy before going. I had been to North Africa just once, to Egypt, and, even though Mauritania was not considered wholly North African, the racism and xenophobia I had seen in Egypt against black immigrants made me wary. How was I going to be treated? My nerves were part of what came with being a black journalist reporting abroad: venturing into places that could be hostile or cold because of the color of my skin. As I left the airport, the city unfolded itself before me through my taxi's creaky roll-up window. After the lush, crowded beaches of Dakar, Nouakchott seemed barren in its sandiness, languid with its calm streets. The place felt marooned in time: aged buildings with faded paint, a few enclaves of elegant homes hidden behind overgrown gardens, and shops and offices that sat in near-stasis amid a thick heat that relented only during the rainy season.

Once a colony of France, Mauritania gained its independence in 1960, and the following decades saw a long series of military dictatorships. The French installed authoritarian president Moktar Ould Daddah, who was then ousted in a coup by a colonel named Mustafa Ould Salek and his junta, who were then removed in a coup by another junta, which was soon led by a colonel named Mohamed Khouna Ould Haidallah. In 1984, he was kicked out, too. Colonel Maaouya Ould Sid'Ahmed Taya was of the same mold as his predecessors, but he relaxed the political climate, allowing political parties to operate even though he continued to dominate successive elections.

In 2005, Colonel Ely Ould Mohamed Vall, Taya's one-time ally and security chief, deposed him; three years later, General Mohamed Ould Abdel Aziz, former chief of staff of Mauritania's army and an advisor to Vall, staged his own coup. Each man said he wanted to end Mauritania's totalitarianism and guide the country into an open, democratic future. Each man repeated the repressions of the one before him. Aziz, still the president when I arrived in the country, had yielded little power to the opposition.

Pervasive corruption enriched Mauritania's tiny oligarch class, while ordinary citizens grappled with the effects of a government that appeared to have little concern for them. Slaves were the most neglected of all. They were not restrained by chains, but they could not go to secular schools, or religious schools, or study Islam in any kind of meaningful, independent way. And because most White Moors perceived Islam as endorsing slavery and taught that interpretation to Haratin, questioning slavery was tantamount to questioning Islam. When slaves were told that servitude in this life brought reward in the next one, some believed it. No one in their community who looked like them had ever known another way of life. How could you believe anything else? One former child slave told me, "The slave is chained to a mentality that outside of their masters they are nothing. In the village, when a slave says he does not want to be a slave anymore, people will ask, 'Why? Who are you? Your mother was a slave; your grandmother was a slave. Who are you?'" Their masters, on the other hand, were the embodiment of Allah's likeness. "To the slave, his identity is his master," Biram said. "The master is his idol, one he can never become, and he is invincible."

It was true that slaves could technically tell their masters that they wished to be free, but slave owners used physical abuse and death threats to keep them enslaved. Nothing belonged to you and yet you belonged to everyone, anyone who had lighter skin and White Moor blood and more education, more money, more things. Everything good was before you, around you, and you were not allowed to touch it, or to desire it, and better to not even think of it. And then there was the biggest hurdle to freedom: defying religious teachings and societal pressure in order to believe that you could be free. How could you think you would be the one, amid the wreckage of the destroyed people you knew and loved, to leave your bondage behind?

Since before he was born, Biram Dah Abeid's family lived as nomads near the Senegal River in the south of Mauritania: raising sheep, goats, and cows and moving by seasons. In the rainy season, they crossed the river to Senegal for verdant farmland, and then came back to Mauritania in the dry season. "It was a very traditional setting. I was not born in a hospital and there was no midwife or doctor," Biram recalled. Their female neighbors had helped his mother give birth to him. Their house was just a tent they could pack and carry from place to place, but Biram was happy.

He was the second youngest of thirteen children. His mother, Mata, had two sons who were born blind, and she prayed for another son until, nine children later, she had Biram. Before having him, she had visited several White Moor marabouts, Muslim spiritual teachers believed to have special powers, and each one promised to make her pregnant with a boy if she gave them enough money, animals, and other gifts. After every visit, she had a girl (once even twins). When she finally gave birth to Biram in 1965, years after all the visits, each marabout naturally claimed credit. His mother nicknamed him Aïnine el Iyil, which means "the eyes of the boys," and his parents cherished him.

Before he was old enough to start school, Biram mostly followed his mother around as she gathered vegetable seeds and animal skins, from which she would make traditional mats to sell in the market. Sometimes he helped her herd their animals. When he was only seven, he noticed that there were two kinds of people. He saw people around him who seemed to own other people, and who could make them do whatever they wanted. The *abd*, or slave, meanwhile, was always hungry, he noticed, and had few clothes and belongings of his own. The men and women looked tired and weak.

Biram's mother was known in their small community as someone who would help when those in need came by their home. One day, a young slave named Mohamed visited. "He was very strong, very young, and very hungry," Biram said. His mother fed him and let him sleep. Later that day, Mohamed's master followed him to their tent. He hit Mohamed repeatedly and led him back to his own home. Biram was shocked. "Why didn't Mohamed react? If he beat him, he would kill him," he told his mother.

"No, he cannot do that," his mother said. "He has chains."

"Where are the chains? I don't see chains," Biram said.

"No, they are in his mind," she replied. Biram's mother explained to him that people had put into Mohamed's head that it was his providence to be a slave, and so he could not react to anything his master did.

Another day during his childhood, a woman in her

twenties named Mediem, the slave of a man who lived nearby, was out herding her master's animals. When she did not return before dark, the master went looking for her and found her having sex with another slave in the bushes. Furious, he took a piece of wood from a fire and branded her genitals. The woman was left very ill. Biram's mother took care of her for weeks. Biram couldn't stop thinking about what he had seen. He was filled with pity for the slaves.

When Biram was eight, the rains began to come less and less, and his family settled in a nearby speck of a town called Jidrel Mohguen. His village had a police post and administrative offices of the local government, a small market, a mosque, a few shops, and not much else. The White Moor families lived in attractive houses on one side of the village. On the other side, the Haratin families resided in houses made of mud. In his own mud house, there were just two rooms and no doors or toilets, Biram recalled, laughing. Everyone in his family was forced to be close.

After selling in the market all day, Biram's mother would stretch her aching arms and legs at home and talk to Biram's father about how the local administration favored the white families. Biram listened to those conversations, and he watched at school as white children went blameless after fights with their black classmates, while the headmaster punished the black students. White Moor students received more attention from his teachers, and had their own school-organized events and treats. The school's administrators were all white and friends with the parents of the white students. Even the few black administrators in town seemed to be co-opted by White Moors; they also showed a bias for the white families. "Our village was divided into two parts, like apartheid. That is when I started to see what discrimination was," he said. A few of his older sisters did domestic work for wealthy White Moor families. White Moors owned the land, and Haratin farmers worked it and gave them the best of their harvests.

Biram's father, Dah, was now elderly and had stopped working, and spent much of his time in the house. He liked to rail against the injustices that occurred in their village. "He stayed angry about slavery until the end of his life," Biram recalled. Dah pushed his son to be aware of the inequality. "That's why he sent me to school," Biram said. He was the first one in his family to go. Though his mother did more to help slaves, she was not as critical as his father. She still thought slavery was fair. But she had empathy for slaves, while Biram's father exuded bitterness. "They were opposites," Biram said. "I think I inherited the two things: my father's desire to act against slavery and my mother's compassion." His mother was extroverted and had helped people as far back as he could remember: orphans, the homeless, and the mentally ill. His mother was so generous that they also called her their mother. Yet his father kept things inside, stirring. He told the slaves who came to their house, with controlled rage, that they did not have to return to their masters.

Biram had a large extended family in Jidrel Mohguen, with many cousins. The police often harassed them. The children did not understand why at first. "I started to see deeply the face of slavery," Biram recalled. "They minimized us, they minimized black people. For them, blacks were not people." One evening when Biram was eight, a White Moor policeman came up to him and his brother, who was blind, in the street. They were playing music from a radio, and the policeman told his brother to turn it off. His brother refused, and he and the officer shouted insults at each other. The next morning, the policeman came to his house and asked for his brother. Biram's aunts, uncles, and cousins grabbed the policeman, pushing him away from the front door. More police arrived, and they were all put in jail. Biram was left reeling; he felt a profound sadness. "I started to ask my dad about the discrimination I saw in the village, and that's when he told me his story," he said.

His father told Biram that he had been born to a slave, and that Biram could have ended up a slave, too. But while Dah's mother was pregnant, her master had fallen ill. Appealing to the Koranic idea that acts of benevolence will be rewarded, the master released Dah from slavery before he was born and gave him his freedom. His mother and older brother remained slaves of the master's family.

As a young man, Dah crossed the river to work for a time in Senegal, where he could live free from racism. Back in Mauritania at the age of forty, he met a woman who was a slave, and they had two sons. Emboldened by love, Dah went to his wife's master to ask for his family's freedom so that he could take them to Senegal. The master refused. "They are my property," he told him. Dah went to court, but the judge told him, "This is his slave—unless you want to buy her from him." He did not have nearly enough money for the price. Desperate, he asked if he could at least take his sons, but the judge refused again. The children are property and don't have a father, the judge said. He next went to the French colonial governor, who told Dah that the dispute fell under Islamic law and that he could not interfere. Dah was defeated. He left his wife and children and returned to Senegal. He vowed to never again fall in love with a woman who was enslaved. A friend later promised to set him up with someone. He took Dah to his home village in Mauritania and introduced him to the woman he would marry, Biram's mother, Mata.

Biram was stunned by his father's story. He told Dah he wanted to do something. As he grew into a teenager, Biram questioned why slavery existed and why Haratin were treated like second-class citizens. "I remember the discussions I had, not just with students, but also with teachers, about discrimination and slavery. My whole life has been filled with these kinds of discussions. But they were not open to understanding and helping me," Biram said. Instead, he felt that most people, white and black, hated him for his questions. His childhood friend Hamady Lehbouss, a bookish, scruffy teacher and antislavery activist, described Biram as unusually fearless. Biram listened to pop music and flirted with the girls at school. But parents warned their children not to spend time with the boy they said was spreading foolish ideas.

When Biram was fifteen, his parents sent him to a diverse high school in the southwestern city of Rosso. His sisters cried when he left home; they didn't want him to go. He lived with a friend of his father who worked for the electric company. At school, Biram started reading Rousseau, Voltaire, Diderot, and Garvey, and he compared the status of Haratin with what he was reading. "I realized we were no different from the people we called slaves," Biram said. He noticed that most of the people in Rosso were black, but the government was white. Haratin didn't seem to be treated like full citizens. He felt himself being careful around White Moors. He composed manifestos on the oppressive situation of Haratin, and distributed them unsigned around the school before students and teachers arrived in the morning. Biram enlisted his friends to write out copies. But Biram's white friends distanced themselves from him. Biram was frustrated, though he felt no remorse. It was simple: They were supporting the unjust system.

At sixteen, Biram decided to stage his first protest. He tried to recruit both Haratin and Afro-Mauritanian students. He told his friends that they had to take a stand against the apartheid in their country like the intellectuals he loved: Césaire, Senghor. He told them that White Moors had all the power, and they had to do something about it. Most of his friends balked, or said they would show up and didn't; it was too much for them. No one could change the situation, they said. But a few agreed to join Biram. In the end, there were about ten of them. Before classes started one morning, they threw out Biram's tracts in the hallways and wrote graffiti on the walls in red paint: *Apartheid*, *No to Slavery*, and *No to Racism*. The white elite in Rosso interpreted any action against slavery as an action against them. When students began streaming into the school, Biram and his friends gathered together and chanted the phrases with which they had stained the walls. Students and teachers watched them with bewilderment and disdain, but Biram had never felt so exhilarated. Like it or not, people had to hear what he was saying. An hour later, security guards broke up the group.

Biram left for the University of Nouakchott to study law, but after a year and a half, he ran out of money. He had barely enough to pay for his bus ticket to university in the first place. And the university's dean already disliked him; he accused Biram of leading student protests for better services on campus. (He was participating, of course, but not organizing them.) Biram took an administrative job in Nouakchott's state court system, decent-paying work he would continue for the next ten years. The courts, like most public institutions in Mauritania, often tilted in favor of White Moors. So throughout the decade, he led demonstrations against what he saw as corruption among White Moor politicians. Many represented districts made up of Haratin whose interests they ignored. When he was twenty-two, during one such demonstration against the imposition of a white mayor in his hometown, Biram hit one of the mayor's supporters in anger to rally his fellow protestors. Biram and his views became well known in the village after that. But slavery had just been abolished in the country six years earlier, with no means to hold slave owners accountable, and few saw Biram as a serious threat.

In the late 1980s, because of his troublesome extracurricular activities, the government sent Biram to Nema, an arid city in the southeast with a burnt-orange terrain. Biram knew he was being punished, and he felt lost and powerless after the move. He needed time to think about how to rebound. Soon after, a case of slave inheritance arose. A slave had died, and the head of the local tribunal wanted to give his possessions to the slave owner instead of the man's family, a standard practice. Mauritania is an avowedly Muslim country, and though the constitution endorses both secular and religious law, in civic matters, like slave inheritance, Islam reigns. Biram, who worked as an assistant at the court, protested. "I was shocked at my boss's decision. He seemed like a good Muslim," Biram said.

And so in 1990, when he was twenty-five, Biram asked to be transferred to the northern metropolis Nouadhibou, a flat city on a peninsula with a port opening to the Atlantic Ocean. The waters that surround the port are a graveyard, filled with abandoned ships left to decompose by owners who want to avoid the costly process of dismantling them. Biram worked at a court not far from a local high school. On his way to work, he passed the school and would often see a pair of sisters making their way inside. They were both beautiful. The first of the sisters he had the opportunity to meet, he thought, he would marry. He was lonely living by myself in the city, and tired of chasing women. He wanted to feel settled.

One afternoon, Biram was having lunch with a friend at a restaurant when one of the sisters, Toutou, walked in. It seemed fateful. He was already infatuated with the fresh-faced, bright teenager, and he hadn't said a word to her yet. He courted her, taking her out and meeting her parents. They ended up marrying and having two daughters. Only later did Biram understand that Toutou's middle-class Haratin family was ambivalent on the issue of slavery. His wife's younger sister and mother did not support Biram's activism and, in his eyes, turned his wife against the important work he was doing. The tension in his marriage was becoming unbearable. Biram was so involved with helping the destitute people who brought cases to the court that more people would visit the tribunal asking for him than for the tribunal head.

That happened a lot with him: At school, now at work, he took on the role of the leader, even if it wasn't his place to do so. He was too impatient to deal with bureaucracy and hierarchy. People would ask for the chief at the tribunal, meaning Biram, and the actual chief became angry. He told Biram that he didn't have the skills to be anything more than his assistant, and so Biram quit.

Biram had always hoped that he would finish his university degree. He would have to sell his car and other possessions, leave his children behind, and divorce his wife—the last of which he felt had become necessary. It was an unhappy marriage. "I realized that my wife did not share the same values," he said. "The most important value to me was fighting slavery, and I wanted to feel coherent within myself. I left everything behind and started over." He began his first year at university in the capital again, almost as if the past years had never happened, though he maintained contact with his ex-wife and daughters.

After finishing his bachelor's degree, Biram, now in his thirties, went to Senegal to obtain his master's. He decided to write his thesis on slavery. As he prepared to start his fieldwork in Mauritania, everyone told him to get in touch with a prominent early abolitionist named Ahmed Khlive. Biram's father had died during his first stint in university, and Biram missed him and thought about him all the time. He wanted to acquire all the education his father never had the chance to get. "My father had the same ideas I do, but not the same means. I will never forget his physical and moral capabilities, but his intellectual limits pushed me to get what he did not have," he said. Biram began reading the teachings of Muhammad, which seemed to him to be clearly against slavery. He read books of Western philosophy that supported this conviction. Locke on liberty and equality, Rawls on justice. "My problem is not against religion," he went on. "It's against the interpretation of religion as the origin, the justification, and the legitimization of slavery. The *use* of Islam, not Islam."

While researching his thesis, Biram was meticulous, interviewing activists and religious scholars to explain why slavery was un-Islamic. He also spent time with current and former slaves. The work consumed him. "I wanted to learn about the mind-set of the slave and the mind-set of the slave master because I wanted to understand how to deconstruct the ideology and how to develop a solution against this mind-set," he said. Biram believed that all slaves knew there was something wrong with their situation, but they lacked the language to explain to themselves why. The slave master behaved as if he were the intermediary between his slaves and God, as if he were responsible for their salvation, making slaves utterly dependent on their owners. He was also the mediator between his slaves and the government.

Biram's research felt like disappearing into an ever-deepening well without knowing when or how he would get out. In the beginning, his siblings did not understand his fixation. Nor did many of his friends. It was isolating. He was looking for a community, other people who shared his convictions. When he met Khlive in Nouakchott, he felt like he had finally found someone who understood him. Khlive treated him like his prodigy, and like his son. For most of 2003, he and Khlive stayed up nights talking about the history of slavery in Mauritania. The men would get so wrapped up in their work that Biram sometimes stayed until morning, sleeping on his mentor's couch. When Khlive left for work, his teenage daughter Leila made tea for Biram and they also talked for hours on end. "He had principles; he was clearly fighting for human rights," Leila told me. Her grandmother had been a slave, and she shared his zeal.

Biram seemed intent on, obsessed with, arming himself—intellectually, emotionally—for an attack on slavery. But he asked Leila to marry him, and she agreed. Leila was fair-skinned with a full, cherubic face that often appeared innocent and distracted, especially when she was accompanying Biram to his speeches and meetings, now that people were beginning to know him as an activist. She wore pretty, floral hijabs and put on heavier makeup than she needed to, but still looked improbably young beneath it, a naive idealist thrust into the role of supportive wife too soon. Whenever Biram was away, she was expected to rally their supporters and keep morale high, which was not always easy to do. "He would only talk about one thing: the fight against injustice, the fight against slavery. Sometimes I see him in the middle of the night or during the day, and he is absent. I ask him what he's thinking about, and he says he's thinking about how to win this fight. Even if it's just he and I together, we don't talk about anything else," she said, shrugging a little. "For another person, it could be a big deal, but for me it's not. I am engaged in this fight. I am with him and I support him."

After finishing his master's thesis, Biram worked for the antislavery organization SOS Slaves. It was the only abolitionist group in the country, started by a former slave. He also wrote weekly editorials for an Arabic-language magazine. But he was growing frustrated with the abolitionist movement. "We were missing something in the fight against slavery," he said. Many slaves, isolated by geography, illiteracy, and poverty, did not recognize the possibility of a life outside servitude, of a life of freedom. Part of Biram's mission was to make them aware. SOS Slaves wrote statements and tried to persuade the imams to denounce slavery, with little success. Demonstrations attracted less than fifteen people. "We needed something more popular, more open, with more action," he recalled.

In 2008, Biram founded the Initiative for the Resurgence of the Abolitionist Movement, or IRA. "We set out to do a civil resistance like the ones led by Martin Luther King and Mahatma Gandhi. The other organizations respect the imams and the books that are the origin of slavery. We don't respect them. We've started a real war with the imams and these books. That was new," he said. Biram attracted supporters with his fiery bluntness; there would be no polite statements from him. He decided IRA would do whatever was necessary to amplify their cause. When the police denied them permission to lead protests, they would hold them anyway.

To free slaves and to force the government to imprison slave owners, IRA began holding sit-ins, staging hunger strikes, and marching through cities and towns around the country. "We are always protesting something," Brahim Ramadhane, one of IRA's vice presidents, told me. Brahim, a gregarious high school philosophy teacher who wore glasses and rumpled suits, had become involved with the beginnings of the Haratin activist movement in the late 1970s. In the early days, the movement was mostly underground. Ramadhane was later working in opposition party politics when he began to hear people talk about IRA, and he read editorials Biram wrote. He realized his work in politics was not enough. "Haratin need to be people first, need to be free first, need to have a place in society first," he said.

Brahim decided to join them. IRA members often drank sugary Mauritanian tea like addicts in his home's simple salon, where a mouse ran around with impunity. When they came over, his children brought out big pots of rice and meat that the men dug their hands into as they lounged in a circle. It was a respite from the scalier side of their work. Sometimes during a protest, the police would beat the activists or spray them with tear gas. The government reacted to the protests in one of two ways. It imprisoned activists, or it put slave owners in jail, only to release them within days and close the cases. After demonstrations, IRA sent press releases to supportive human rights organizations in Europe and the United States, and circulated them within the Mauritanian diaspora.

After IRA was founded, authorities dismissed the organization and accused Biram of being an attention seeker. Policemen taunted him, saying that the president had told them not to arrest him and to let him do whatever he wanted. "Whenever we brought a slavery case to the police, they would release the slave owner," Biram recalled. "We would tell them that they were criminals, and they said, 'Say whatever you want.'"

In October 2010, activists heard of a slavery case in the southwestern city Rosso. They did what they always did: piled in cars and went to find the slaves to bring them to the local police station. Even though the slave owner, when the police summoned him, admitted his wrongdoing, the police refused to jail him. "I decided that this had to stop," Biram said. "The next time we had a slavery case, the police had to put the slave owner in jail or put us in jail."

Two months later, in December, Biram learned that two girls were being held as slaves in a wealthy quarter of Nouakchott. That evening, he called together about eighty activists, and the group went to the house where the girls lived. He also called the police. An officer showed up at the house with dozens of policemen and said they would take over. He told the activists to go home. "I told them we would not leave until you free the girls and put these criminals in jail," Biram said. He knew the police would likely just accept whatever the girls' masters said to them. The policemen blocked the front door, while the slave owner and her sister cowered behind them.

After several minutes, the police finally took the girls to the station, and Biram and the others followed. For a moment, the activists—schoolteachers, civil servants, students, out-of-work intellectuals—were in a standoff with the police. Biram walked toward a policeman. When the policeman grabbed his shirt, Biram butted him twice with his head. "I wanted to go to jail," he said. "Because it would be the one opportunity for us to inform the world that there is slavery in Mauritania. When people ask why I am in jail, they will have to know there were two girls who were enslaved, and the government refused to put the slave owner in jail."

As the activists and the police clashed, Biram lunged at the policeman again, and he was arrested. He was sentenced to three months in prison; the slave owner was released after nine days. While in prison, he heard that the president had said that he forgave the activists and was going to release him. The activists responded that they didn't want his forgiveness. It was IRA's first victory. The police jailed a slave owner for the first time. They considered that day the birthdate of the organization, the point at which their struggle began to have an impact.

Over the next four years, IRA would help put about twenty other slave owners, including members of some of the country's most powerful families, in jail, though often for brief terms. As owners heard about the arrests, they started releasing their slaves in a ripple of fear. Working through a network of 9,000 activists, IRA succeeded in freeing thousands of slaves around the country. Haratin took to calling the former slaves *Biram Frees*.

In April 2012, Biram arrived home in Nouakchott. It was Friday, the holiest day of the week, and he was enraged. When he landed at the airport, he was welcomed by Leila and their children, along with hundreds of supporters who filled the peeling, sweltering box of a terminal and swelled into the parking lot, where taxis idled under trees waiting for passengers. Biram was now the most prominent antislavery activist in Mauritania. He had forced the government to put another slave owner in prison a few months earlier. Now he had learned that the man was released after less than two months in jail, despite being sentenced to two years for working two young boys without pay and abusing them. Biram had felt shock, and then deep disappointment, when he heard the news of the man's release.

Now forty-eight, Biram had the directness of someone with little to lose. He had hooded eyes, a heftier build than that of his youth, and a warm demeanor: intim- idating but fatherly. Before his arrival at the airport in Nouakchott, he had been in Europe to meet with human rights groups that were supporting his work fighting slav- ery, and which had sponsored his travel.

On his way home from Europe, Biram stopped in Senegal. While there, a fellow activist called him in his hotel in Dakar. A Saudi Arabian imam had been on of- ficial Mauritanian radio, Biram's friend told him, and the imam had encouraged sinful Saudis to buy Mauritanian slaves and then free them. This act would absolve them of their sins. Wealthy Mauritanians were known to bring slaves to Saudi Arabia as gifts to colleagues and acquain- tances, as if they were toys. Rich Saudis even bought Mauritanian slaves as child brides.

On another evening in Dakar, he turned on an Arabic- language television channel. A well-known Mauritanian imam, Mohamed El Hacen Ould Dedew, was giving an interview. The journalist asked Dedew if slavery existed in Mauritania. The imam said no. Then why, the journal- ist asked, had Dedew recently given the journalist's boss a slave girl as a gift? Dedew simply smiled. Biram was in disbelief. Dedew, a high-profile member of the Islamist political party, was obviously lying, and had no shame while doing so. It couldn't be a coincidence that these events had occurred so closely together. It seemed like a sign—he needed to do more. "I decided to give the state of Mauritania a lesson," he said.

Biram paced his hotel room, thinking. For the last few years, he had been trying to devise a way to scare slave owners who were shielded by the government. Mauritania kept agreeing to international resolutions banning slavery, but within the country, the government claimed that Islam sanctioned the practice. Biram sat down on the hotel bed and called other IRA leaders. He instructed them to buy from the market several books on Islamic law. Biram next called another IRA member, who was an imam, and asked him to speak at that week's Friday prayer about the falseness of the jurisprudence books. The imam agreed. Then Biram hung up; he didn't tell them what he was planning.

The Koran is ambiguous on the essential question of whether slavery should exist. In much of the world, Muslim scholars argue that the only Islamic basis for slavery is in jihad: After conquering unbelievers, Muslim warriors could take them as slaves, provided they treat them well. In Mauritania, there was not much agreement. Imams who defended slavery referred to a set of texts that dated as far back as the eighth century. One prominent example was a *mukhtasar*, or handbook of Islamic law, written by the fourteenth-century Egyptian scholar Khalil ibn Ishaq. According to its rules, a slave could not marry without her master's permission, nor did she have any right to her children; a free man who murdered a slave would not be punished by death, but a slave who murdered a free man would; slaves were whipped for fornicating, though a master could rape his slave; and slaves could not inherit property or give testimony in court. Slaves were not human, they were nothing more than things to be owned and used.

When Biram boarded his plane to Nouakchott, he was so nervous he couldn't eat the food they offered him. *I have to do this,* he thought over and over. He and Leila drove home from the airport, his children squirming in the backseat. He changed from his pressed suit into a traditional Mauritanian *bubu,* a long and loose embroidered tunic, and then went to the Riyadh quarter, a section of the city with rocky lots, narrow sand-bleached streets, and pastel-painted concrete houses. A few hundred people had assembled under a bright sun. Men sat cross-legged on a wide mat on an empty stretch of street, wrapping their turbans tight to ward off dust. Women and children gathered behind them, some sitting on a bench. Activists, residents, and the press had been alerted; this would not be a normal Friday prayer. The imam and a procession of activists stood and gave speeches attacking the legal books. One man said the Islam practiced in the country should be called "Islam made in Mauritania." Another man said he was not against Islam, just against any interpretation of the religion that violated Islam's principle of egalitarianism. Yet another called for a Haiti-like slave revolt. A plainclothes policeman sprang up and shouted, *"Allahu Akbar!* What you are saying is wrong!" Men escorted him away. Many of the speakers would be arrested in the days following the public prayer, and some would end up leaving the antislavery movement altogether after harassment from the police and government.

At last, Biram came to the microphone, his face set into a look of determination. He spoke like a preacher, moving and rousing, reflective and provocative. There was no room for anxiety now. Reporters pushed voice recorders in front of him. "Today will be a historic day. We will begin today to clean the faith of Mauritania; we will purify the slaves and the slave owners, because both need to be purified," he said in Hassaniya, the local Arabic dialect. "There is a group of bad people who are guarding Islam and using it however they want, and that group is dividing society, putting some people on top and some people down—not because of what they are doing or who they are, but because of the color of their skin. We will stop that today." He predicted that the government would undertake a violent campaign against the activists and their supporters after the prayer. It had already targeted them in the past. But today would be the beginning of the end of slavery. The crowd murmured in agreement.

Biram addressed the government of President Mohamed Ould Abdel Aziz, the former military officer who took power in a 2008 coup. "Start your campaign against me," he went on. His voice rose to the point that he was nearly shouting. "Say that I am against religion, write that and say that in your mosques, give money to your slaves and send them to say that everywhere, that will not help you. What will help you is when you go back to the truth. They cannot say the truth. They cannot say that there is slavery here, that there is corruption, that there is racism," he said. The audience watched, transfixed, as he condemned the authorities. "We don't have to explain ourselves to them. We are not afraid and we don't need their money. Sometimes we have water for dinner; we don't have any money to have lunch or dinner. But we are not afraid." He paused, the kind of silence that was both contemplative and deliberate. "If we die, it will be from the front, not the back. We will not run away."

He called President Aziz an ignorant military man with whom it was pointless to negotiate, and said that religious leaders were little better. For years, Biram had asked the Supreme Council for Fatwa and Grievances to prohibit slavery. He would not ask anymore. IRA would free slaves on its own. "Where are my books? Where are my books? Where are the books on slavery?" he said suddenly, snapping his fingers. There was a flurry of activity as some IRA activists, rangy young men in sunglasses, scrambled for the legal texts. "These books justify selling people, they justify raping people. We will purify the religion, the faith, and the hearts of Mauritanians. What the prophet says was hidden by these books, which are not real words from God. These old books give a bad image of Islam. We have no choice but to take this step." He was holding a red hardcover book covered in intricate embossing.

One of the young men dropped the books into a cardboard box. He doused the box in lighter fluid. The crowd was now on its feet, trying to get a good view of what Biram was doing. No one had expected this. Defacing the holy books of Islam was a crime of apostasy, punishable by death.

Biram set the books on fire.

3

NIGERIA

No Regrets

IN 1976, when Abba Aji Kalli was eleven years old, he stole his grandfather's tractor. To Abba, taking the tractor felt like the most natural and essential thing to do at the time. His grandfather, Abba Aji, his namesake, worked for the Nigerian ministry of agriculture and was out of town on a business trip. Someone needed to go supervise the work at the family farms and collect the day's earnings— why not Abba? He walked through the tractors parked in the garden of his grandfather's house in the northeastern city of Maiduguri, the capital of Borno State. A skinny stalk of energy, he bounced with excitement. Each time he had the chance to ride as a passenger on one of the tractors, he watched how his grandfather or one of the farmhands maneuvered the vehicle, how they steered it on the scrub-edged roads.

On the day after his grandfather left for the central state

of Bauchi, Abba chose a tractor, took a nail, flattened it into a shape that would fit into the ignition, and started the engine. Within a few minutes, he was on Damboa Road headed to the countryside, where the ground began to sprout in thick, springy bushes and bendy grass. It was the first time he had ever driven anything. He felt like he was floating through the air, a god above everyone else. He was small but the tractor made him feel powerful, like an adult who had to be respected.

Once Abba arrived at the first farm, not much more than twenty miles outside of town, he gleefully drove it up and down the rows of rice, maize, and millet, digging and moving and unloading like he had seen done so many times. The land stretched before him in an array of browns, yellows, and greens, lumpy dirt and dense weeds and leafy crops under a gleaming, swollen sun. He passed some of the hundreds of cows they owned. The farm workers watched him with amusement but didn't stop him. He gathered the money from nearby farmers who were renting his grandfather's tractors into a pouch, just as he had seen his grandfather do. In the early evening, he drove the tractor back to the city.

When Abba arrived home, his grandfather's older sister, Aisha, was waiting for him. Whenever his grandfather was traveling, his grandaunt came to help his grandmother take care of the children. His grandfather had three wives, as allowed by local Islamic custom, and they, their children, and grandchildren lived together in a spacious compound. His grandaunt stayed at his grandfather's first wife's house, where Abba and other grandchildren lived.

They were all terrified of Aisha. She was impossibly tall, and an unrelenting disciplinarian. If Abba got out of school in the afternoon and caused mischief with his friends in the streets, she would wait at the gate to the house and yank him inside, shouting the whole time.

When Abba returned home from the farms that evening, Aisha asked where he had been. She seemed tense but calm. He told her about what he had done with the tractor, and about going to the farms, and about how he had collected the money. He was being much braver than he thought he could be. He tried to not visibly shake. Aisha quietly told Abba to hand over the money. After he did, she began screaming. How could he have done something so stupid? She reached for him, but he fled her grasp. He ran as fast as his legs could take him and hid until she went to bed, and then he slunk around the house after that. He avoided his grandaunt at meals, but after three days, her anger seemed to have subsided. He thought she probably even appreciated what he had done. He forgot that he had taken the tractor without permission.

When Abba's grandfather returned from his trip to Bauchi, he told Abba to come see him in his room. As Abba arrived, his grandfather seemed upset, and told his grandson that he should not have taken the tractor. He demanded to know where he had learned to drive. After Abba informed him that he had taught himself and that he didn't need any supervision, his grandfather beat him so badly that Abba had trouble walking for the rest of the day. It didn't weaken his enthusiasm for what he had done, though. He would do it all over again. He was proud of himself. He secretly knew he had been right to do something when no one else could.

Abba grew up as one of nineteen brothers and sisters, but he always felt chosen and special. His father, Modu, was a prosperous cow trader and farmer, and his mother, Fatima, his father's fourth wife, looked after the children. He had four brothers and six sisters, and another nine half siblings from his father's three other wives. His father had a vast cement compound of semisecluded, connected cottages and rooms; Abba's was painted a brilliant turquoise. It was near a rust-colored villa with sweeping archways called Shehu's Palace, the official homestead of Borno State's traditional ruler. It was also close to Abba's grandfather's home.

Maiduguri was a hot and sprawling city of several hundred thousand people, laced with open-air markets, serene residential and business quarters, and streets teeming with hawkers and minibuses. You could walk freely in most places and feel safe, even as a little boy. The 1970s in Nigeria was a time when, if you were poor, the government would pay for your medical treatment if you were sick. You could get a scholarship to an excellent school. A high school graduate could easily find a good position. The Nigerian naira was on par with the British pound. Nigeria was so wealthy thanks to its newly exploited oil wealth that it almost didn't matter that billions of government dollars were disappearing.

Abba was outspoken and stubborn, and especially close to his sisters. He was the firstborn of his mother's children and behaved like it. He didn't want to lord his status over his siblings, but circumstances, well, encouraged it. After his mother finished breastfeeding him, her parents decided they wanted to raise him themselves. He was their first grandchild, and it was not uncommon for children to be raised by extended relatives in a close family. They brought him to their house, and Abba grew up happy. "Nobody could even shout at me or discipline me in the house," Abba recalled. "Whatever I needed, he just bought for me. Even if I did wrong, he didn't punish me." His grandfather still had some of his own children living with him, but Abba was doted on and adored. When his clothes were dirty, a houseboy assigned to take care of his needs washed them. His meals appeared in front of him whenever he was hungry, and he had his own room.

When Abba was still eleven, his grandfather's younger brother Kalli, worried Abba was becoming too spoiled, came and took him while his grandfather was away on a work trip. When his grandfather returned home in the early hours of the morning and learned what his brother had done, he immediately went to his brother's place. "Do you want to stay with him or come back with me?" he asked Abba. His grandson said he wanted to stay with Kalli, who was once a ranking soldier in the military and now worked as a vehicle inspection officer. Abba's young female cousin, a toddler, was also living at his granduncle's house and was sick. Whenever Abba was around, she held on to him and allowed him to feed her, something she wouldn't allow anyone else to do. He felt it was his responsibility to stay in his granduncle's home until she had better health; only he could do it. His granduncle still spoiled him anyway.

Abba's grandfather died in a car accident the following year. Abba was distraught at the death. He clung tighter to his granduncle. When Abba turned fourteen, Kalli began making plans for him to study in England. He had picked a reputable boarding school and obtained a passport for his excited grandnephew. Kalli was going to enroll him for the next school year when he returned from a trip to Saudi Arabia. But when he came back, he was rushed to a hospital. A few days later, he died of liver disease. Abba was left with a kind of pain he hadn't known was possible.

The men who had been his fathers were gone. He felt left behind. He continued to do well in English, math, and science at school, and he dutifully kept playing on the soccer team and participating in the military cadet program. But after his granduncle died, Abba's grandaunt took him back to live in his father's house. Children, his brothers and sisters, roamed through the compound, rolling around in the courtyards and in the living rooms, draping themselves over couches and beds, huddling in the kitchens and the gardens. He wasn't the chosen child anymore. He was just like everyone else. Even his mother, Fatima, felt like a stranger. He hadn't seen her much over the years, and when he did, he referred to her as his sister. His grandaunt had been raising him, and he considered her his mother. When he returned to his father's house and asked which woman was his mother, his grandaunt started crying. "This is your mother," she said, pointing to Fatima. Abba was confused by her emotion. "This is who gave birth to me?" he asked. His grandaunt told him she had. "So I had to adjust myself back to the conditions in which I found myself," Abba said. "Because the world had come to an end for me at that time."

He loved watching *Hawaii Five-O* and Bruce Lee movies at home, but at school, other students knew him as being somewhat rigid. His grandfather had taught him to never lie, that it was a losing game, and he took the advice to be his guiding principle—even if it meant getting his classmates in trouble. The local police thought of him as a good, reliable kid who they could call if they needed information about trouble involving the students. "That's why people didn't like me!" Abba said years later. "Because I don't hide things." He rarely thought about the consequences of what he said. As long as he was honest, he reasoned, whatever happened was meant to happen.

His father believed in Islamic education and had put Abba's siblings in madrassas. Abba kept going to public school, but he was the only one out of all the children attending. His singular status set him apart, made him feel lonelier. When Abba reached high school, he managed to persuade his parents to allow several of his brothers and sisters to start going to school with him. His father was already letting him attend, so what was a few more children?

After Abba finished high school, in 1985, he started working for his uncle. Now twenty, he helped run the business sorting, packaging, and selling gum arabic, a natural material found in products like soda, candy, pill coatings, and cosmetics. The work was fine, but unfulfilling. He had little time for himself, much less to play soccer anymore. Two years later, Abba met a girl named Yagana. He first saw her at a high school sports tournament; she was still a student. Yagana was quiet and kind. She liked reading and taking walks outside. She was calming. When they began their life together, after she graduated, Yagana devoted herself to him, and he loved her dearly for it. Their first child died of pneumonia at three months, but they soon had another daughter and two sons.

After five years in the gum arabic business, Abba looked for a civil service job, a stable, well-paying career in Nigeria then, and found a position as a clerk in the auditing department. Four years later, he enrolled in a polytechnic college in Maiduguri, where he studied accounting while continuing to work. When he graduated, he was promoted to auditor. But his marriage was coming apart. He and Yagana separated; Abba had just begun his thirties. He struggled to understand what went wrong with his marriage, which lasted less than six years. "I took good care of her, and she did take good care of me," he said. But he realized that she wasn't happy. They quarreled. Yagana couldn't tell him why she was miserable—she wouldn't explain—and so they parted ways. Abba wanted things to be his way, and he sometimes couldn't see around that. He was out of sorts for a while, unable or unwilling to recognize his part in the ending of his first love. The children stayed in his custody, except for their daughter, who went with her mother.

When he was posted to the town of Shani in 1997 to

work in the auditor's office there, Abba met his colleague's younger sister Hamsutu. She filled the room: She liked to talk, and tell jokes, and play music loudly. They fell in love, married, and he brought her back to Maiduguri, where she got a degree in community health and found work in a government-run clinic. They would have eight children together. Abba married his second wife, named, like his ex-wife, Yagana, in 2002. He had been conflicted about taking a second wife. He appreciated the way Hamsutu supported him. But he had been taught all his life that, in case his first wife became sick or left him, a second wife was essential to keeping the family going. Most Muslim men in northeastern Nigeria did the same, or believed in the idea. It was ordinary to have a family with multiple wives living in close quarters, or on the same street, teaching and feeding each other's children, helping each other financially, and fulfilling their lives together. He would end up also having eight children with Yagana.

Abba was drawn to his third wife, Aisha, who was adventurous and curious about the world, while he was having problems with Yagana, and she briefly moved out. They married in 2011 and would have three children. And so, over the years, he formed a small army: six girls, fifteen boys.

As busy as he was fathering children, Abba kept working. The central auditor's office in Maiduguri sent him to branches in towns and villages around Borno State, where he stayed for up to a few weeks at a time. His job was to make sure government funds were accounted for, and that no one was misusing them. He relished being an instrument of justice, a necessary check on the moral corruption so prevalent in Nigeria. How could someone steal money meant for other people, for the public good? He had always wanted to guide the people, be chosen by them, and lead them when others wouldn't. Eventually very few people would call him Abba. He would become the kind of upright person he knew he was destined to become. People would look up to him, ask his advice. Everyone would know him as Elder.

When Rebecca Ishaku was a young girl in Chibok, her favorite game was called *saraya*: You had to play it with a group of other children, and as everyone sang, you gathered together and tossed one person high in the air, catching her as she came back down to the ground. Another of her favorite games was *bulubu*, where you attached a string to an object to throw it as far as you could. She relished the act of release, freedom from all restraints, and then the fall to safety.

Rebecca liked to wear her hair in a tumble of tiny braids, usually under a head scarf made of a bright *ankara* fabric, sometimes decorated with hearts and polka dots, that matched her dress or skirt and blouse. She was slender, shy but luminous, with high cheekbones and a disarming smile. When I first met her in 2015, she was nineteen and her voice barely went higher than a whisper; later it began to rise and boom with the energy of a teenage girl who had a lot to say, and not many people to say it to. Her skin was a light, warm brown, and she was fond of wearing tiny silver or gold hoops. In contrast to her stylish, though modest, traditional outfits, beach flip-flops usually adorned her feet. Her English was getting better and better; in Chibok, she loved to sing in her first language, Kibaku. It was an uncommon language, spoken by just the residents of her town and surrounding areas, an area of less than 70,000 people. It wasn't surprising when members of a group called Boko Haram arrived and couldn't speak it at all.

She was born in 1994 in the general hospital in Chibok, a farming and trading hamlet about eighty miles from Maiduguri where pedestrians, motorbikes, and cars converged along the sleepy main drags. The crowded roads were lined with stalls and shops. Their owners talked and laughed amid transactions, nestled under wide, bright umbrellas or sitting behind counters with the doors flung open. Rebecca grew up in a compact house with three bedrooms in a village just outside of Chibok called Mbulabam, in the foothills of the pale and brown stones of the Mandara Mountains. Mbulabam was surrounded by rocky escarpments covered in golden weeds.

Rebecca was the third youngest of eleven siblings, four sisters and seven brothers. "There were a lot of us—too much," she said, laughing. They shared everything among them. They even took in her four cousins after Rebecca's uncle died. Some slept on mattresses, others on sheets on the floor. They invented games, sang and danced to drums they played, helped each other with homework—especially math times tables—and prayed together. She spent much of her time with her little brothers Peter, Noah, Adam, and the youngest, also named Peter. ("I don't know what my father was thinking," she said. They called the youngest Wabi, "Peter" in Kibaku.) She fought them playfully and disciplined them when they misbehaved. "I was very, very happy," Rebecca said.

Her mother, Saratu, and her father, Ishaku, both worked as farmers, and they grew enough food for the family to live on, but not much more than that. Her father was fair but exacting. "My father was very kind, but sometimes, if you did something he didn't like, he would be very hot," Rebecca recalled. He, without fail, wore black loafers, an embroidered cap with a flat top, and a chunky watch. He put on a sweet-smelling cologne that she liked to inhale deeply when he pulled her in for hugs. In the evenings, he settled into the couch or in a chair at the dining table and turned on the radio to listen to the news. Her mother, short and curvy, was a devoted churchgoer. She loved to sing, and her voice filled the house. She was a patient listener and gave Rebecca advice when she needed it.

Her community was intimately connected. If a family didn't have enough food, their neighbors would help them until the next harvest brought more to eat. Nigeria had been pieced together in 1914 and then controlled by British colonialists until its independence in 1960. It was loosely divided along religious lines: a mostly Muslim, ethnically diverse north and an ethnically plural, predominantly Christian south, though there were many exceptions to that rule. Chibok, a northern town, for instance, was heavily Christian. Under British rule, the north was governed via local emirs, preventing interference with the region's Muslim identity, while the south was more directly ruled by the British. The north remained largely agrarian; the south eventually developed an economy centered on oil. Because Christian missionaries were concentrated in the south, southerners also had access to Western education. The regional differences persisted: Literacy rates were significantly higher in the south, while poverty was more entrenched in the north.

All the children ran in and out of everyone's homes in Chibok, and all the parents knew the other parents. Even before she started school, Rebecca wanted to help the people in her area, to become someone of importance. But the rule in Chibok was that you couldn't enter school until you stood taller than the height of a man's arm when he stuck it straight out. So she didn't start school until she was ten. She received her school uniform, a blue dress with a matching hair tie, and took care to make sure it was always pressed and clean. As she progressed through the grades at her elementary school, she excelled in English and math and decided that she wanted to be a lawyer. She played volleyball and javelin, read storybooks and later novels, and liked to dance.

Maybe because she had entered school later than her classmates, she seemed a little young for her age, the dreamy, innocent one content to gather her best friends Comfort and Sarah in the shade of a tree, and tell them stories as they made up their own world.

In 2001, a young, passionate cleric named Mohammed Yusuf began preaching not far from where Elder lived.

Elder once went to hear one of the sermons. Hundreds of people were in attendance, folded together in a court- yard as Yusuf spoke in front of a house. Elder was im- pressed with what he heard. "He was saying what God has said!" he recalled. Yusuf talked about how Islam prohib- ited murder and stealing, and how the religion promoted transparency, goodness, and righteousness. Elder agreed with all those things. He considered Islam to be important in his life, and he prayed every day. "People at the time were saying this man is a very good man, that he is telling the truth," Elder said. He had known Yusuf when he was a child, and Elder was in his twenties, and thought he was brilliant. Yusuf had gone to Koranic school and spoke English. He was a serious and quiet man, slim and unas- suming. He and Elder greeted each other when they met in the neighborhood. At Elder's wedding to his second wife, Yusuf even gave a speech. Some of Elder's friends had invited him. Yusuf spoke about how God wanted couples to live well together, and to provide for their chil- dren and give them good educations.

But suddenly, Yusuf's preaching began to change. He was telling people not to go to Western schools or courts of law, and to abide by Sharia. He tried to put this idea into practice among his supporters: He settled disputes, set up marriages, and arranged loans. He spoke about jihad and creating an Islamic state. He blamed the govern- ment's failures—graft, high unemployment, inadequate schools, poverty—on Western civilization and education, which he said corrupted Nigerian leaders. He was quickly gaining followers, though Elder wasn't as moved by this new Yusuf. "I had seen so many people like him," he said, self-announced prophets who became popular for a time by claiming that only Islamic law could provide for the welfare of the people.

Things were different now. You had to know someone important to even get a decent job. Men of Elder's generation were among the last to benefit from the country's oil-driven economic expansion after independence. Some followers turned away from Yusuf, but many stayed with him as others joined. They agreed that a fundamentalist interpretation of Islam was necessary to repair the country. His supporters consisted of disillusioned young men, who ranged from the jobless to top graduates of the University of Maiduguri who burned their diplomas in solidarity.

Over the next years, the group, then known as the Yusufiyya movement, attempted to create settlements free from government interference in neighboring Yobe State and then later back in Borno State. When members moved back to Maiduguri, local media had started to call them Boko Haram, which translates to "Western education is forbidden" in the regional language, Hausa. But the group's official name had become Jama'atu Ahlis Sunna Lidda'awati wal-Jihad, which means, in Arabic, "People Committed to the Propagation of the Prophet's Teachings and Jihad." As they were harassed by security forces, Boko Haram cells attacked police in the northeast, killing officers and taking their weapons. Northern politicians were said to have employed the group in its beginnings to intimidate opponents.

When another clash in 2009 between the group and

security forces resulted in Yusuf being detained and then killed by the police while in its custody, Boko Haram revolted. After Nigeria's independence, a succession of military governments had held the north and the south together, suppressing ethnic and religious differences and quelling dissent. Civilian rule returned in 1999, renewing hopes of a more equitable society. Nothing changed. The benefits of the oil wealth were still going to the elite, widening the gap between the rich and the poor. Extremist Islamic groups filled this moral vacuum, as they often had in northern Nigeria. But Boko Haram did more than that: It successfully started a war by promising redemption through insurrection.

With a vicious, angry man named Abubakar Shekau as its new leader, the group, now numbering a few thousand fighters, began burning down schools, police stations, clinics, and other government buildings. Yusuf was thoughtful and charismatic, but Shekau, a former theology student, seemed psychotic, determined to sow violent chaos for the fun of it. Boko Haram members destroyed water sources and power stations, and blew up cell phone towers, markets, and churches through central and northern Nigeria. The group funded and armed itself through bank robberies, arms trafficking, private donations, extortion, raids of Nigerian military barracks, and, allegedly, al-Qaeda affiliates that also trained some of its fighters. But after Boko Haram raided a community, like the fishing town Baga in Borno State, killing residents and soldiers, the army then arrived in the area and proceeded to burn down houses, beat and execute men and women, and even throw children into fires. The military behaved as if the victims of the attacks were the orchestrators of them, or as if they were in league with the terrorists because they shared the same religious and ethnic backgrounds. Nigeria's armed forces were some of the best trained in Africa, but the soldiers stationed in the northeast were often from elsewhere in the country, had little connection to the people they were supposed to protect, and were, understandably, afraid of dying. They had inadequate weapons and gear because their generals siphoned the country's $6 billion security budget and benefited from the ongoing war. Soldiers endured low salaries and rations, and had little morale.

But the soldiers had it wrong. "When Shekau descended into this mass, random, indiscriminate slaughter, killing people for no reason, a lot of people didn't understand what was going on and did not ascribe to the philosophy of the current leadership," Fatima Akilu, former counterterrorism adviser to the government, told me. And so Boko Haram began to rely on intimidation to grow their numbers, kidnapping thousands of boys and young men.

Boko Haram focused its onslaught on Elder's hometown. Once an ancient center of Islamic teaching and trade, Maiduguri was, by 2013, a city of sandbagged bunkers and security checkpoints that disfigured its streets. Soldiers manned the bunkers and checkpoints and stood in the roads, guns cocked, monitoring traffic. Sometimes the soldiers wore balaclavas; most of the time they appeared to be barely wearing any protective gear at all. Sections of the city were reduced to rubble.

The attacks were unpredictable and chilling. In June 2011, Boko Haram bombed a beer garden; it also set off bombings at markets and police stations, and on crowded stretches of streets. Boko Haram attacked civilians seemingly at random, ripping into their homes, killing their parents, stealing their daughters and sons. "It really hurt me," Elder recalled. "But we were handicapped, we couldn't do anything. We were even afraid to report it to the military or authorities, because if you report it, a few days later Boko Haram will just come and kill you." This was not the Nigeria he knew. This was not the Islam he knew. This was something different, and terrifying.

People Elder knew began to flee town; his friends were killed. In 2012, one of Elder's cousins was shot in the leg by Boko Haram gunmen when they encountered him at his house. The cousin had been sitting outside, enjoying a moment of free time. He soon left the city with his family. A friend of Elder's, a state assemblyman, visited Elder and his family one day that same year. Elder later learned that his friend had been shot in his house right after leaving Elder's. And, to make matters worse, his brother's own son had joined Boko Haram. When the insurgency began in 2009, his nephew was attending Yusuf's sermons, and he ran away that year from Maiduguri. Everyone knew he had joined the group.

There was no sound logic behind the killings. They killed you if they thought you worked with the government, or sometimes if you worked at all, or if you had your children enrolled in school, or if you were simply

trying to live your life and take care of your family. Elder
felt helpless. At any point, you could hear gunfire close to
your own home. No one was safe. Even if you survived a
Boko Haram attack, you then had to make it through the
military roundup that followed. After an attack, the insurgents dispersed, often hiding among residents. Soldiers
swept through neighborhoods detaining every boy and
man they saw, taking many back to a military base outside
of town called Giwa Barracks. The road to the base was
long and windy, nearly deserted, through beige sand and
dirt and skeletal trees.

They even took Elder from his house once, in 2011,
and beat him. A soldier hit him on the head with a gun
so hard he was bleeding. He had to get stitches. Looking back, Elder said he couldn't blame the military for
what they did. The people weren't providing the soldiers with information about the insurgents, so what did
they expect? They couldn't just hide terrorists and not
expect the military to react after so many of their own
had been killed. He had forgotten how scared he and his
neighbors had been to report on Boko Haram: Either the
group could have found out and retaliated against them,
or the military could have accused them of being terrorists themselves, and taken them.

Elder had become used to death: the idea of it, the
presence of it, the inevitability of it. It was all around him,
all the time, a sticky, sour thing that he could touch and
smell and feel. It was not supposed to be like this. Everyone was afraid of Boko Haram, but no one wanted to talk
about them, much less risk reporting them to the military.

If you saw members on the street, you walked past them and said nothing. Boko Haram extorted business owners and white-collar professionals, regular payments they had to make to stay alive. They paid without protest. There was nothing else to do.

So it surprised everyone when, in June 2013, a mild-mannered taxi driver named Lawan Jafar apprehended a Boko Haram member in an area of Maiduguri called Hausari. With a few other men in tow, Jafar went to the home of a man he believed was involved with the terrorists. They found him in possession of a gun, and turned him over to the security forces. News spread of the citizen's arrest. People talked about how Jafar was a hero, a simple man who had done something even the military couldn't do. It was inspiring. Men, and some women, in other quarters then banded together.

Elder considered Jafar a would-be martyr who had truly sacrificed himself, and enviably become a leader in the process. He set out to emulate him. His neighborhood was the fourth to join. "We knew the Boko Haram members who were living in the neighborhood with us. We just started getting them in the night. We would catch them and then bring them to the authorities," he said. He was the oldest of the group he joined up with back then, a loose association of men who lived near each other. They used sticks and cutlasses to defend themselves.

The very first day, they went after three young men, named Shehu, Usman, and Bukar, who they suspected of being militants. The suspects all lived with their parents in the neighborhood. Elder and the thirty other men were organized. They headed on foot to the suspects' houses. At the first house, they didn't find anyone. At the house of the next one, they found all three of them together. The relatives of the second man were also there. They watched, stunned, as Elder and the group crashed into the main room and tied the hands of each man behind his back, and then led them outside. "They didn't say a word," Elder recalled. "Because they know the habits of their boys." He told the young men that he knew who they were and what they did with Boko Haram. The suspects were laughing. They had tried to run when Elder and the rest came in, but had nowhere to go. They had known the vigilantes would be coming after them, but seemed to be in a state of disbelief. The men said they weren't the only Boko Haram members in the area. They started calling out names, people Elder and his group would pursue in the following days.

The three men then said they had made a mistake joining the insurgents, but Elder barely listened. He didn't care about their regret or remorse. "I didn't have sympathy for them whatsoever," he said. The next morning, the men's parents came to the vigilantes and begged them to release their sons. Elder refused; he said he had turned them over to the military. He hadn't heard news of them since.

Now, any place where residents knew Boko Haram members to be living, the new militias gathered together in groups of ten or fifteen, piled into a vehicle, and took suspects by force. When people heard what they were doing, hundreds of men and boys joined them. And terrorists began fleeing town. Within a week of forming, the vigilante groups had cleared the city.

The neighborhood groups organized themselves into ten sectors with command structures, and they called themselves the Civilian Joint Task Force. The CJTF, as it was known, was made up of volunteers—professionals, civil servants, students, and traders armed with machetes, locally sourced guns, and other homemade weapons. Elder was made a unit commander, eventually leading 8,000 men. A kind of initiation process developed: Each member had to swear his allegiance on the Koran. Most, like Elder, belonged to the Kanuri and Hausa ethnic groups, the same groups that made up most of Boko Haram.

When officials with the Borno State government first learned about the civilian fighters, they invited the CJTF leadership to a meeting of their security council, headed by the governor. CJTF leaders were asked about their mission and practices, and they responded that they only wanted to apprehend terrorists and hand them over to the military. Faced with a worsening crisis, the security council decided to recognize the group as a "voluntary organization." The government gave the vigilantes vehicles, uniforms, and stipends on the condition that they participate in an army-run training program.

Elder began renting an office to run sector five. He was the only sector commander to do so. The auditor's office had given him a leave of absence for this new public service, while still paying his salary, and so he wanted things to be official, to be run properly. From the time he woke up to when he finally fell asleep, still restless, Elder responded to calls alerting him to terrorist sightings, impending or ongoing attacks, and recent abductions and killings. (A mobile phone operator once called him to ask why he used its service so much.) Elder thrived on the danger, and on the responsibility of having the fate of lives in his hands. His own life and work had suddenly acquired a meaning he had never imagined possible. He didn't show his fatigue, and was relentlessly optimistic about their chances of defeating Boko Haram. And so the boys under his direction, and the people around him, began seeing him as both commander and father figure, a sliver of light to follow in the darkness.

Elder was the one who caught his eighteen-year-old nephew and brought him in. It had to have been him. When he heard the boy had come back to Maiduguri, he went looking for him, and found him with AK-47s. To Elder, the guns were proof that his nephew belonged to the terrorists. But his nephew went further; he confessed to killing more than thirty people, and even threatened to kill Elder. "I asked him, 'Is this the way we brought you up?'" Elder recalled. "You know, the first thing before you start this job, you will take an oath. The oath is that you will not hide anybody, whether it's your friend or relative." Elder was the first of the family to see him when he returned, and the last person to talk to his nephew before he took him to the military. It hurt Elder to see him that way. He was Elder's family, his blood. Now what had he become? Elder refused to accept that his nephew could be rehabilitated. His mind was polluted and his actions were unforgivable. His betrayal enraged Elder. "We have no regret for anybody if you are a Boko Haram member, because we have suffered a lot at the hands of Boko Haram," Elder said. "We have lost so many people." He watched the military execute his nephew with satisfaction. Elder's brother had said little at the news that Elder had so swiftly caught his son, turned him in to the authorities, and then watched him die.

His brother must have been upset, I said. "No, he was not upset," Elder said quickly. And his brother's wife? "Nobody was upset in the family, because anyone who brings destruction to the community, we will never stay with him," he said. But his brother refused to talk to me; he said he didn't want to revisit his son's death. Elder eventually admitted that his brother did feel bad that "his own blood had joined this type of people." His brother and sister-in-law had been forced to watch their son turn into someone they didn't recognize.

In high school, Rebecca's roommates included two girls named Saraye and Saratu. They did as much as they could together, having meals, reading, even going to the showers at the same time. While only girls boarded at the Government Secondary School, boys came to classes during the day and then went home. Rebecca watched them with a tentative curiosity. They weren't allowed to date, but some of her friends liked the popular, good-looking ones; she couldn't even imagine talking to them. They were so loud and rowdy. "I was very shy," she said. "The boys were too silly; they would talk and tell jokes while the teachers were trying to give lessons, and disturb you when you were listening."

The school was interfaith, and Rebecca had both Christian and Muslim friends. She was also the secretary of a Christian student group. She liked to read the Bible, and found solace in reciting prayers with the other girls. Her faith was what remained steady through everything: leaving home, moving to a new school. God was who she knew would always be looking out for her, guiding her when she didn't know what to do. Praying comforted her, like rolling up in a mound of cool sheets and burying herself inside.

She generally tried to stay out of trouble, particularly since "some people liked to fight," Rebecca recalled, no matter what you did. One afternoon, after washing some of her clothes, she hung them up on a line outside the dormitories. When she walked by the line later that day, she realized someone had come to the line, gathered her clothes, and set them on the ground. She watched a girl put up her clothes in the same place where her own had been. "I asked her, 'Why did you pack my clothes and put them on the ground?'" Rebecca recalled with a tiny smile. "She shouted, 'Are you stupid? Do you know me?'" The girls started fighting before Rebecca knew what was happening, falling to the ground, punching and kicking. A teacher soon came to pull them apart, and Rebecca went back to her room. She was embarrassed and ashamed, but also a little defiant. She didn't want to be someone who was afraid to stand up for herself.

In 2010, when she was sixteen, Rebecca first heard of

Boko Haram. The group was waging war in Maiduguri, setting off explosions, assassinating politicians, and killing ordinary people. She heard about two boys who were abducted and taken to a terrorist training camp. She felt a vague sense of worry. Rebecca still felt sheltered enough in Chibok, but wondered how long the walls around her home would hold.

A few years later, Boko Haram raided the school in Damboa, about twenty miles away, burning the school to ashes. Some of the surviving students were sent to Rebecca's school to finish the term. Their classes bulged with the young, traumatized girls. "I was very afraid when the girls came," Rebecca said. "I thought Boko Haram would follow them to our school." Every night, Rebecca prayed that God would protect her and her classmates. She wished that she could even go home after class every day and sleep in her childhood bed, but she tried to be brave. In February 2014, Boko Haram attacked another school in Yobe State, where it shot and slit the throats of fifty-nine boys, and told the girls to get married and never return to class. Rebecca prayed that her little town on the edge of Sambisa Forest, a vast scrubland of thorny trees and bushes, would be left alone.

On a Sunday morning in 2014, one of Elder's contacts called from Yola, a small metropolis on the Benue River and the capital of Adamawa State. The contact said a suspected Boko Haram member was returning to his home in Maiduguri. Elder guessed that the young man was coming to pick up supplies, maybe weapons he had stashed somewhere. He gathered his boys and dispatched them to the suspect's house in one of the unit's blue pickup trucks.

A few hours later, I met Elder for the first time at a hotel in Maiduguri that was popular with the military and relatively secure. He was now a wiry, energetic man of forty-nine who was balding and wore rectangular gold-rimmed glasses. He had a salt-and-pepper beard and a gruff, scratchy voice. Elder favored slim slacks and short-sleeved button-down shirts, tailored in the same color or print. He had with him three men who had all been seized by Boko Haram. Sometimes Boko Haram compelled the boys and men it captured to spy or fight for the group; sometimes it killed them, a warning to anyone who would collaborate with government forces. The men with Elder had managed to escape, and I had wanted to hear their stories.

While we sat talking in one of the hotel's offices, Elder's phone rang. As he listened, he became agitated, twitching with excitement. "We got one," he said, hanging up. His boys had captured the Yola suspect. Elder told me he had to go and rushed out of the hotel.

Two days later, I met him again at one of his two homes in Maiduguri, a modest bungalow. The power was out, and his third wife, Aisha, lay on the floor with their young children, fanning them as they napped. I joined Elder on the couch as he pulled up the cell phone video he shot of the suspect. A young man in black athletic shorts and a red T-shirt appeared on the screen, surrounded by men shouting questions at him. He couldn't have been much older than eighteen, and he looked dazed. "He confessed that he was a member of Boko Haram, and that they have been hiding AK-47s in one house," Elder said gleefully. He, his boys, and another sector commander told the suspect to show them where he had stashed his weapons. At the first house he took them, they dug in the yard and didn't find anything. At the second house, still nothing. At the third, they found two AK-47 magazines.

When it was over, they handed him over to the military. He had fled Maiduguri when the vigilantes started chasing Boko Haram out of the city. Now, many members were living in Abuja, Nigeria's capital, 500 miles away; some were hiding in Lagos, the country's biggest city; and others were living in Kano, the largest city in the north. During their first official operation a year earlier, Elder and his boys had captured ten suspects with AK-47s. All were turned over to the military and detained. More recently, they had apprehended nearly forty people they suspected of being Boko Haram members in Abuja. With each mission, Elder's unit had become increasingly adept at rooting out militants. This time, the entire operation, he boasted, had taken less than thirty-five minutes.

I asked him about the guns his crew was carrying. They looked like relics from the nineteenth century, short-barreled muskets with wooden grips. Residents of the city donated money to help buy the weapons, he said. Their cutlasses and sticks couldn't fight militants armed with antiaircraft guns and rocket-propelled grenades. Elder bought the locally made guns himself, and distributed them among his boys. Their area was one of the most dangerous. His zone covered the outskirts of Maiduguri almost up to Sambisa Forest. "Anything can come through us," he said.

Later, I followed Elder to the small office he rented near the post office. When I visited, stacks of bags and boxes of donated items—clothing, shoes, dried goods—for victims of Boko Haram attacks filled much of the space. After greeting the men in his force hanging out in front of and inside his office, he took a seat at his wide wood desk and began rifling through papers and taking calls. Elder was frustrated with criticisms of the CJTF. He believed that anyone who was uneasy about them must have a relationship with Boko Haram. "We have done a lot to bring peace to this city," he said. If his neighbors refused to understand that he was trying to help them, he would make them understand. When Elder spoke like that, it reminded me of the way Boko Haram had also tried to forcefully convince Nigerians, through violent chaos, of the justness of their cause.

Several boys marched into Elder's office, saluting him before sitting down to wait for their training stipends. Among them was Mohammed Musa, an electrical engineering student at the University of Maiduguri who had signed up with the CJTF a year earlier. For the young men, joining the group was a way to reclaim a sense of power after so much had been lost: relatives, friends, schools, a viable future. He said that his parents were happy that he volunteered, but he recognized that much of Maiduguri was wary of the civilian force because it was imposing its own law and order. "Many people fear us," he said. "They say, 'See this Civilian JTF, they're doing bad things.' They act as if we're useless or up to no good. They should be praying for us every day."

Elder's son Lawan, a small-framed and polite seventeen-year-old in his last year of high school, entered his father's office and slid into a chair. He told me how he inspected cars at checkpoints and carried a knife for protection. One criticism of the CJTF was that it recruited children—another thing it had in common with Boko Haram.

The military's abuses of the people had waned once the vigilantes established themselves, Elder said, because the CJTF kept them in check. But Amnesty International released footage in 2014 showing what appeared to be Nigerian soldiers and CJTF members near Maiduguri cutting the throats of suspected Boko Haram members and then pushing them into an open grave. The human rights organization said the vigilantes had made arbitrary arrests and engaged in torture and extrajudicial killings of suspects, both independently and with the military. To the Borno State government, the vigilantes, as the governor put it, were a "divine intervention," but he admitted human rights violations could have occurred.

None of this was easy for Elder. He didn't accept any of the allegations. He couldn't. He knew some things had gotten out of control; he wasn't blind. His boys were zealous—they all were—in this fight to keep their families safe. But those reports of torture and murder couldn't happen under his watch. He didn't think much of anyone who decided to join Boko Haram, but he wouldn't tolerate those kinds of actions. As for his colleagues, he knew less about what they would allow. Or maybe he did know, and it was easier to think he didn't. But he wasn't a terrorist. He was nothing like Boko Haram. It was not a simple thing to govern a bunch of boys, especially those who were uneducated. "We are not using any children. If we see any underage ones on the streets, we arrest them and call their parents," he said. "We don't kill anybody. We hand them to the authorities. We have to protect ourselves, but we normally catch them alive."

Still, when he tried to tell his boys to do the right thing, they didn't always follow his orders. He sent them on patrol; at times, he wouldn't find anyone at work. What if an attack had happened during those hours? The thought drove him mad. They did manage to show up with their problems. Sometimes the state government could help with money or medicine, sometimes it couldn't, and the burden fell to Elder. "The pressure is too much on me," he said. He didn't have time to read, to play sports, even to eat. He was constantly on call, waiting for a message that would tell him where the fighting was, where he had to go, and who he had to bring. What kind of weapons he needed.

On the morning of April 14, 2014, Rebecca woke up at six. She went to the showers, dressed, walked to the common hall for breakfast, and then to her art class to take her final exam. Exams were beginning that week, and though she had barely enough time to study for all her classes, she had been able to sneak away the day before to see one of her older sisters before she got married. The ceremony was going to be that day, and Rebecca was excited for her sister. After the art exam ended, she and the other girls headed back to their dorm, already celebrating. They jumped onto their beds and danced, talking over each other and eating candy and boasting about how well they thought they had done on the test.

Later that afternoon, some girls settled into their desks to study, and Rebecca went to pray with the Fellowship of Christian Students. On the way back to the dorm with her friend Saraye, the girls took turns quizzing each other for their government exam. That evening, she slid into her bed with her government book in her hands. In her half-asleep haze, she could hear her roommates laughing at the sight of her clutching the textbook as she slept. She dreamed that she was in a car with one of her brothers, and they were driving on a bad road through the bush. Other people in the car were crying; when she asked her brother why, he told her because Paul, her older brother, had been killed. "It was my dream that something bad would happen," Rebecca said. She shouted in her sleep. Her roommates leaned into her bed, grabbing her and asking what happened. Before she could answer, they heard more shouts from outside. Rebecca looked out the window. There were dozens of men, young, rough in appearance, wild-eyed. They were wearing military uniforms, but as they came closer, she saw them carrying heavy weapons. They didn't look like normal soldiers.

"You people come outside! Come outside!" she heard them shout in Hausa, which was commonly spoken through the northeast. It was late, around ten at night. A few guards had been stationed in front of the school, but Rebecca could no longer see them. The men were breaking into the dorm. The ones not in uniform wore black shirts and covered their faces with cloth. One entered their room and stood between the beds. He ordered the girls to gather their things and come with him. Rebecca was in a stunned daze. While the others went outside, she packed a bag. Her brother had just given her beautiful black fabric that he had bought in Lagos, and that she hadn't even had tailored yet. She put that and some clothes in the bag. She slipped on sandals. "I didn't know what was happening," she recalled. When she and the other remaining girl finally went outside, a man was standing in front of the dorm waiting for them. He was holding a grenade. "You want to go with a bag?" he asked her incredulously. "Okay." He took it from her.

Rebecca started to feel dread: A realization was edging to the surface. When the men began shouting *"Allahu Akbar,"* she was sure. They were Boko Haram. The man holding the grenade told her everyone else had gathered at another point, and then led the two girls to where more than 300 of their classmates shivered under trees in front of the school. Some of the men went inside to loot supplies. As the other girls cried, fighting to breathe, Rebecca couldn't move or feel anything. Three weeks prior, she had had her appendix removed. She thought briefly about that. The wound hadn't healed yet. One of the men approached her and put a gun to her head. He said her time had finished. She responded, still in a daze, that if God wanted her time to be finished, then so be it. If not, then she would live. The man lowered the gun and asked where the storeroom was located; they wanted to take any food in there. As Rebecca and another girl led him to the room, he asked them why they had come to school.

"We are here for studying," she told him.

"Which studying?" he said dismissively. Rebecca kept quiet. "You know this studying you are doing is forbidden," he said. "We will burn your entire school." The two girls begged him to spare their lives, and to just destroy the school.

"You are deceiving yourselves. You don't know that you are pagan?" he asked.

The girls didn't say anything.

"Do you repent?" he demanded.

They remained silent.

Back outside, gunmen took the food—macaroni, noodles, spaghetti, rice, yams, and flour—to load onto their pickup trucks. Rebecca felt a surge of bravery. She asked aloud that since she and her classmate had led them to the storeroom, could they and the other girls leave now? "Who asked you to say anything? Keep your mouth quiet," one of the men shouted at her. A classmate whispered to Rebecca that the men were animals; they couldn't be reasoned with. When the last men emerged from the red-roofed cream buildings, they lit them on fire. The men then threw the girls' belongings into the flames.

As the girls listened, the militants began to debate about

what to do with them. Rebecca had imagined herself getting away, all the girls running into their parents' houses again. She saw now there was no chance of that happening. One man said they should finish the girls, just kill them. Another one suggested killing them one by one. Yet another said that their religion did not allow them to kill women. As the men argued, some of the girls were sending pleas for mercy into the silent sky. Rebecca had no tears. "My mind wasn't for that place," she said. "I told them crying wouldn't help, that it was better to pray. Maybe God would save us." Finally, it was decided: All of the girls would go with the men. No one would be left behind. One man said that he would eventually free them, but that he would make them suffer before letting them go.

So they trekked through the forest, past unlit villages where residents knew not to come out of their houses. The girls were careful not to trip or stumble because they knew the men would hit them if they did. The men told them not to run, or they would shoot them. When they reached a series of parked trucks, the militants pushed Rebecca and the other girls onto the truck beds. They were crammed so tightly that there was no space to sit. Her classmates were still crying. After the students squeezed onto the trucks, there were four girls remaining. A man told the four of them that if they repented they could leave. Rebecca couldn't see in the dark if the girls repented or not. But the man went on: "When I open my eyes, I don't want to see the four of you here. Go and tell the parents that we came and kidnapped their daughters." The girls ran.

The trucks began moving, trundling through the foliage, snapping leaves and crushing bushes. Tree branches whipped the girls as they passed. One girl fell, twisting her leg. Rebecca and the others held her as she moaned in pain. Rebecca whispered to her friends to stop crying. One of the men heard her and asked why she was speaking. Did they want to die now? She started praying. "You're praying to your God. You think your God will save you?" he taunted her. Rebecca prayed harder, struggling to focus on her words. She opened her eyes, and looked out of the truck with a sudden clarity. She couldn't follow these men. She didn't know where they were taking them, how long they would keep them. It scared her to think of what they would do to them.

She had to jump.

4

SOMALIA

War and Basketball

AISHA RECEIVED her first call from the terrorists when she was fourteen. One day in 2013, she was at home in Mogadishu, Somalia, when she looked down at her phone to see that an unknown number was calling. She picked up. Islam does not allow women to play sports, the man on the other end said, nor to wear shirts and pants. It was immodest and indecent. His voice was harsh and threatening. He told her that he was going to kill her if she didn't stop playing basketball. The next day, another man called to say the same thing. He would kill her, too, if she didn't stop playing.

The calls were relentless. Aisha changed her phone number three times, buying a new SIM card from a nearby shop and giving the number to just her family and closest friends, but the calls kept coming. She realized there must be someone working at the mobile phone company who gave the callers her contact information. Her cousin worked at the phone company, and he told her that whenever she saw the number of one of the men who called her, she should take it down and then he could trace it back to its owner. But the calls usually came from blocked lines.

After a while, Aisha stopped being afraid of picking up. She argued with the callers. She told them to leave her alone, and that was she going to do whatever she wanted. She said that she was not going to stop playing just because they told her not to play. When they promised to kill her, she responded that only God was in control of their souls. They would not be the ones to decide when she died. She was only a fourteen-year-old girl, but even she knew that, unlike these supposedly pious men. But then her mother started receiving calls. The men told her that she was going to lose a daughter if Aisha didn't stop going to her basketball games. It was *haram*, forbidden, they said, trying to appeal to her faith. Her mother was worried and wanted Aisha to stop playing.

Aisha had first picked up a basketball only recently, but had taken to it quickly. Her phone became filled with photos and videos of the basketball player she most wanted to be like: a famous athlete in America named LeBron James. One of her friends, a sports journalist, talked about basketball all the time and kept mentioning him. She looked James up on the Internet and found his playing mesmerizing. He was powerful and agile, endlessly clever. "He is black and tall and a really nice player," she said. "I like how he shoots the ball." She wanted to have that kind of excellence, and magic.

Aisha's father, Khaled, had worked for a long time as a referee for the basketball and soccer leagues in Somalia, and she went to his games when she was small. Her uncle had also worked as a referee; he had traveled around the world for his job. She was destined for basketball, in a way, like how rural Somalis were meant to be with the camels that gave them everything: food, milk, a way to carry their lives from place to place. "My father encouraged me. Whenever I went to the basketball court and he was refereeing, to see women and men playing, it was inspiring," Aisha recalled.

She joined pickup games in tan-dirt lots around her house with the kids who lived in her neighborhood. She didn't know what she was doing, but she didn't care; it was exciting just to be holding a ball. Aisha started thinking about what it would be like to play on a real court. "I always wanted to play basketball, but I was afraid that I wouldn't find girls who would want to play with me," she said. She had a friend, Leila, who started taking her to a court so they could watch the women's league games. Not long after, she met a coach named Nasro Mohamed, her mother's former teammate, who asked if she was interested in playing regularly. Nasro had started playing basketball at twelve herself, making her way onto a women's team and then coaching children after she retired. Nasro got together Aisha and seven other girls who all had little experience to start practicing.

Mogadishu, Aisha's hometown, was a rambling city that was once beautiful, with pale, handsome buildings that held government houses, mosques, and grand homes, all angling for proximity to the city's white beaches at the edge of the Indian Ocean. Now, after more than two decades of civil war and lawlessness, every building was saturated with bullet and shell holes, or crumbling, or newly built and characterless, and the streets, where sand pooled in the cracks, were filled with soldiers and policemen. In the cafés off the sidewalks, men gathered to talk and argue at all hours, drinking tea, smoking hookah, and chewing qat, the leaf with stimulant properties. Women lingered near them, selling food and drinks from their stalls. They all kept their gaze on the streets, observing passersby and the events of the day.

And so there were always eyes watching you as you made your way through the city, even if you didn't know they were looking. The eyes could be friendly, willing to offer a hand if a suicide car bombing suddenly went off. Or they could be hostile, ready to report you to people unknown. In Somalia, the difference was a matter of life and death. Women knew where in the city to cover themselves with burqas when the eyes around them became intolerant, and girls knew where to pretend that they didn't play sports, had never touched a ball, in order to leave with their lives.

Aisha grew up in a quarter of the city called Suuq Bacaad, where the houses were low, humble bungalows behind bright gates with peeling paint, and she still lived in the same home. She had two brothers and one sister. Her family wasn't rich, but had enough money to never go without. Her father, Khaled, had three other wives and divided his time between those families and Aisha's, but he managed to be with Aisha enough for her to feel loved. Khaled had a peaceful disposition. Every morning that they woke up in the same house, he asked her what she had planned for the day, and he encouraged her to practice basketball. He visited her on the court and took her playing seriously. "My father told me, either leave basketball or aspire to be a professional in it at the international level," Aisha said.

She took for granted being in a family where each member looked out for the others. "My parents really worked hard to make sure I had everything that I needed," she recalled. Even her neighborhood functioned like a clan: She played hide-and-seek—her favorite game—with the other children, some of whom were as close to her as siblings. When Aisha was twelve, her mother sent her to live in the northern city of Galkayo to help her elderly grandmother around the house. Aisha didn't want to go; it was lonely being in a foreign city, and she missed her family. She spent a lot of time by herself in her grandmother's home, and while she was in Galkayo, her attendance at school became erratic.

When Aisha returned to Mogadishu nearly two years later, she soon stopped going to school altogether. She just didn't like it, and was easily distracted. "I was not good with the teachers; I talked too much. I never stopped talking and telling jokes. I love talking. It's my thing. I annoyed everyone in class," Aisha said. "I didn't feel like it was necessary for me to continue." When she attended school, the best part of her day was going with her friends to a nearby court to watch games after classes were over.

Her parents were upset when she dropped out. They had both gone to university and prioritized education for their children. They tried to force her to go back to school, but Aisha refused. And, anyway, there was a civil war in full swing, between the government and Islamist militants, and there was destruction in every place she knew.

Aisha's mother, Warsan, ran a café and a business selling gold. Long before the war, she had also played basketball in her youth, alongside Nasro, Aisha's coach. Warsan was tall and youthful looking. She was kind, never hitting her children like the mothers of Aisha's friends, and she treated her children like people she respected. She provided as best she could for them. When Aisha turned twelve, she asked her mother for and received a cell phone. No one else her age had one at that time. And even though Warsan feared for her daughter's safety, she understood Aisha's desire for basketball because she once had the same need. Warsan only stopped playing once she married and had children.

Other women in Aisha's life were less encouraging. Her grandmother didn't want her to play basketball: She told her granddaughter to keep inside, away from the men with guns. It was too dangerous outside to be so reckless. "Your mother played basketball in the days when everything was okay, but not now," she told her. Aisha also had a very religious aunt who preferred she stay at home. Her aunt wanted Aisha to stop playing so that she could focus on her education. Aisha's older half sister was married and lived in a conservative area, and whenever Aisha went there, her sister's neighbors told her that being a girl who played basketball was against Islam. Her brother-in-law's family

shared the same feelings and told her as much. But Aisha
didn't listen. "We need to go after our dreams and what we
want for ourselves," she said. Even if it ended up killing her.

Somalia ceased to be a coherent state in 1991, when its
dictator at the time, Siad Barre, was forced from power by
rebel militias from several of the country's clans and sub-
clans, which were jockeying for power. When he fell, the
nation fell, too. Barre had assumed the presidency after a
military coup in 1969. He declared the end of the lineage-
based clan, the primal way by which Somalis identified
themselves and wielded power, and tried to impose a so-
cialist nationalism that would unite Somalis on the basis of
citizenship and eliminate the complex, shifting alliances of
clan politics. To that end, he introduced the written aspect
of the Somali language, which had only been oral before,
and a countrywide literacy program. Still, basic documents
that tracked the progression of a person's life, like birth cer-
tificates, went unissued, and it had changed the concept of
time in Somalia. Countless people were "born" on January
1; it was easier to say that than trying to determine, in retrospect, when the actual date had been. Aisha was never
exactly sure about the year of her birth, or about the years
that other major events had happened, too.

After Barre left office, the struggle among warlords
ended when the Islamic Courts Union, a group of Sharia
courts, emerged in the early 1990s out of the lawlessness
and assumed power. They took a harsh view of both
petty and serious crime: Thieves had limbs amputated,
adulterers were stoned, and murderers were executed.

Sports were declared satanic acts. Somalis caught watching matches on television were arrested and sometimes killed. Girls couldn't even go to stadiums to watch basketball, let alone play it. Women felt forced to cover themselves while outside of their homes. At the end of 2006, Ethiopian troops, backed by the U.S. government, invaded Somalia and fought the militias of the Islamic Courts Union, who called themselves al-Shabaab, or "the Youth" in Arabic. They succeeded in pushing the Union's fighters out of Mogadishu in six months, but their abusive tactics against Somalis created support for the young militants who went underground, soon to be joined by foreign jihadis, ready to return. The fighting raged through the late 2000s and into the next decade.

There were still functioning regions, like the self-declared independent state Somaliland, and the semi-autonomous region Puntland, both in Somalia's north. But Somalia was so unstable it became a refuge for senior al-Qaeda leaders, who found anonymity in the chaos. The Islamic State had also begun to move in. The weak central government had a tenuous claim to urban centers like Mogadishu (al-Shabaab still controlled many rural areas), but only by being in business with clan leaders and their militias. The claim was so tenuous that many government officials spent time out of the country, where it was safer, whenever they could. Those who did live in Mogadishu resided in guarded hotels to avoid being assassinated. Their families lived in Kenya or Europe.

Somalia was a facade of progress. Despite the veneer of a federal government and a uniformed army, nothing had really changed. Government officials maintained their offices by paying off the right clan and al-Shabaab leaders to keep what little power they had, and to stay alive. The African Union military mission took back control of Mogadishu from al-Shabaab in 2011, but their soldiers were still getting killed in striking numbers by the militants, and they were reluctant to go on the offensive. Ethiopian soldiers lingered on the Ethiopia–Somalia border, but explosions and gunfights were still occurring all over the capital. The Somali National Army had been trained by Western advisors, but restaurants and hotels were still being raided by the terrorist group. U.S. special forces and drones killed al-Shabaab leaders, but Aisha and other girls were still threatened with murder for competing in basketball, handball, and track and field in loose pants and long sleeves with their hair wrapped up.

Somalia's neighbors Ethiopia, Kenya, and Uganda, all major contributors of peacekeeping troops, were in the war for their own gain: Their governments maintained beneficial relationships with the United States, which gave them aid for carrying out its war on terror and ignored their abuses of human rights and power in their own countries. But after the gruesome murders of eighteen members of the U.S. Delta Force in Mogadishu in 1993, which inspired the film *Black Hawk Down*, the United States was reluctant to send its own ground troops into the country again. It had a lot to worry about in Somalia: The influence of the Islamic State, which was seizing coastal towns, and the failure of the clandestine U.S. campaign in Somalia, which was conducted through spe-

cial forces, airstrikes, and private contractors. Brutal counterterrorism policies, encouraged by the United States,
in both Somalia and neighboring Kenya—which had a
swelling Somali refugee population and had experienced
its own devastating al-Shabaab attacks—had pushed bitter
youth into the hands of the insurgents. Drone strikes, indiscriminate neighborhood raids, and mass detentions of
the mostly innocent had left young people distrustful of
their governments and, in some cases, filled with desire
for revenge. Extremist ideology was an answer to their
alienation.

In Somalia, the absence of governance had created a
peculiar world in which havoc reigned from all sides: The
terrorists and the military were both menaces not to be
trusted. No one really was to be trusted. Somalis spoke
of spies, people listening and watching who could report you to al-Shabaab. They could be your neighbors,
colleagues, friends, or family. The collapse of a social con-
tract that had once let people feel in control of their lives
had wrecked every part of Somali life. Once trust was
gone between citizens and their leaders, it slowly vanished
among the citizens themselves, and then that distrust cor-
roded the bonds even between people who knew each
other intimately.

Somalia survived only because of the energy and re-
silience of a people who endured terror attack after terror
attack near their homes and at their weddings and fu-
nerals, at a breakneck pace that would snap anyone's
neck. Yet they managed to keep going. In 2016, a friend
took me to an outdoor restaurant in Mogadishu called

Beach View on the stunning Lido Beach. The eatery was packed; people crammed each table, laughing, eating seafood, taking selfies. We sat by the edge of the balcony and looked out onto the clean, golden sand where children played and, farther out into the blue-green sea, where families piled into wooden boats for sunset rides. As we left, my friend casually mentioned that al-Shabaab had attacked the restaurant just a few months earlier, killing at least twenty people. They drove a car filled with explosives into the adjoining hotel first, and then ran into the restaurant, shooting. Patrons hid under the tables, in the kitchen; they ran out to the beach, only to die on the sand. But on the evening I was there, I felt no traces of death. The owner had repaired and reopened the restaurant within weeks, and people had come back as if nothing had ever happened. That was how things went in Mogadishu. While they lasted on this earth, Somalis would not be denied the few pleasures it had to offer them.

Aisha was fifteen when the terrorists threatened her in person. They had started by calling with promises to kill her, then they found her. Aisha treated basketball like a job now, and it was almost all she did, going to the court for practice, training for games. After learning from Nasro, she had flitted among teams in the national women's league, looking for one that fit, and had landed at a team called Heegan. Aisha was a center, responsible for handling, guarding, and shooting the ball from the most physical position on the court. There were single girls on her team, married women, ones with children, others who were students. They were nearly all in their teens and early twenties, and talked and joked around with each other like sisters. Some of her closest friends were outgoing, adventurous players named Salma and Bushra.

Aisha was leaving practice with Salma and Bushra one evening, like she did so many times on so many evenings. They hailed a tuk-tuk, one of the yellow rickshaw taxis crashing through Mogadishu's streets, which pulled up to the curb just as they were nearing the street. They entered and told the driver their destination. At one point, the driver, who was on the phone, took a wrong turn and then stopped. Aisha leaned forward and asked him where he was going. He told her something was wrong with the vehicle, and that he was calling for help. Another man approached the tuk-tuk. He was holding a gun. "You girls are infidels; you're not Muslim," the man told them. "You're playing sports and walking on the street wearing pants." He aimed the gun at Salma, and she jumped up. Salma had been a police officer, and she confidently lunged for the weapon. But he fired and the bullet grazed Bushra's leg. The girls managed to call over a policeman, and get out of the vehicle. After they breathlessly told him what had happened, he arrested the men and took them to jail.

Later, the police had a press conference announcing the arrest of the man with the gun. He had admitted to organizing several explosions in the city. Aisha watched it on television. "He is still in prison today," she said with satisfaction. For once, there had been justice. The week after the incident, the girl who sold snacks during games told

Aisha that the tuk-tuk driver had been circling the court while talking on his phone the day he picked up the girls.

Despite the extremists' attempts to repress women in Somalia, Aisha and her friends found ways to feel normal. In her world, "people speak what they feel," Aisha said. If a boy liked her, he told her, and she then decided if she wanted to date him. When she was sixteen, her team traveled to Galkayo for a game. She met a boy working in the Mogadishu airport named Abdullahi. He was twenty-two. When he saw her, he immediately asked for her number. Aisha thought he was handsome, but didn't give it to him. When she returned to Mogadishu, he asked for her number again, and she gave him one she never used. But they later connected on Facebook and he asked her to send him a photo. They talked, and Aisha began to consider what romance might mean for her future. "I believe that I can manage to be married and play basketball," she said. "Because there are girls who married and have kids who still play on my team." A year later, she hadn't told her father about Abdullahi, but her mother knew him. Abdullahi would visit them at home, and sit and talk with her mother over tea. Aisha went with him to Lido Beach.

That was part of the complexity of Somalia: Before the militants, before the extremism, Somalis had practiced their faith with moderation and tolerance, where flirtation and romance were done out in the open and encouraged. Aisha's phone buzzed a lot; it was often another boy trying to court her. She usually silenced the phone with a smile. She wasn't interested. Abdullahi was supportive of her playing basketball, and he came to her games. They could talk about it together. A lot of boys she had met wanted her to stop playing, told her they should get married, but Aisha could never imagine being in a relationship with someone who thought like that. Men like Abdullahi and her father were uncommon, but not extinct.

Still, no one made Aisha feel as supported as when she was on the basketball court. When she was chasing and shooting the ball, she experienced a kind of happiness that felt like it could lift her and carry her away. Everything seemed possible. Playing basketball made her feel like she had accomplished something for herself, like she was worthy enough to be in pants and a shirt, like she deserved this feeling of complete liberty. It was motivating in a way; it made her realize there were better things out there for her, just beyond where she could see. Playing let her not think about her problems for a while, let her go blank and allow her body to guide her. She wanted to get so good at basketball that people knew her name all through Somalia.

But in those early days, she just had to survive. Aisha was leaving the basketball court in Hodan District at dusk with five other girls after practice. Hodan District was known as a kind of dangerous place, where shootings and attacks were common. Aisha was happy that day. ("I'm always happy," Aisha said.) She was wearing a red headscarf over a white blouse and long green skirt. She had to keep her team shirt in her bag when she was outside the court, and her track pants were underneath her skirt. As they were walking, a black sedan stopped alongside them. The driver, a man she didn't recognize, asked the group if they needed a ride, not an unusual occurrence in Somalia. He was middle-aged and wore his beard long. He had on a white *kandora*, a linen robe common in conservative Arab countries. Aisha was on the phone with her mother, who was asking her to pick up milk and cooking oil on her way home. One of the girls asked the man to drop them off farther down the road. Aisha wedged into the middle of the backseat between her friends.

A few minutes after the girls climbed inside the car, the driver pulled to the side of the road and stopped again. There were few people around. He sent a text message to someone and then turned around to tell the girls that he knew who they were, where they were coming from, what they were doing, everything about them. He told each of them the names of the neighborhoods in which they lived. Aisha felt pricks of fear spread through her; her body suddenly felt like it was on fire. He sounded like a militant. "I know that you all are playing basketball," he said. They shook their heads furiously. They all said that they did not play, that they had just come to watch the sport. "I've been watching you play basketball," he went on. "All of you. And I've been following you."

The man's phone rang, and he got out of the car to pick up the call. He locked the car as he exited. Aisha was panicking. The girls tried to unlock and open the doors, but they wouldn't move. They started pounding on the windows. The man came over and rolled down one of the windows so he could watch them as he talked. Aisha pushed herself out of the window and fell onto the rocky ground. She looked desperately around her and then picked up a big stone. She turned to the man and told him that if he didn't let them leave, she would throw the stone at the windshield. She was shaking; she thought that he was going to kill them. "We were all really scared, but I had to do something," she said. "I had to jump from the window. Because if we stayed scared, this guy would kill us. I know I'm crazy but I had to do something." The man said to her, "Now you want to destroy my car? I wasn't going to harm you. Calm down." He unlocked the doors and the girls scrambled out. Aisha hailed a tuk-tuk and they all got inside, sitting tightly next to each other to feel safe. The man had returned to his vehicle and was now following them.

The ride to Aisha's neighborhood took an hour. They stopped for a while to see if the man was still behind them; the girls didn't want to lead him to their homes. When they saw him again, Aisha told the driver to go to a police post. The man left for good once they arrived at the station. Aisha and the others told an officer that a man from al-Shabaab had threatened and then followed them. She told no one else. "I had to hide it from my family so that they wouldn't stop me from playing," she recalled. "I never told anyone, so no one knows." Aisha was sure that if she let on anything to her parents, they would send her to stay with her aunt in Ethiopia or, worse, keep her at home.

Mogadishu was barely like what I expected. I imagined a bombed-out landscape of terror attacks and gun battles, which was true, and I thought people would be confined inside, longing for indulgences they once enjoyed. But before I even landed in April 2016, Ifrah, my twenty-three-year-old interpreter, asked if I could bring her something from Nairobi, Kenya, where I was taking a flight to the Somali capital. Would I mind packing a bottle of tequila? As I bought one in a duty-free store in the airport, the shop employees advised me on the best way to stow it in my luggage to avoid it being detected by the Mogadishu airport staff who searched your suitcases for contraband when you landed. I would have to keep it in my tote bag because, as it dawned on me, alcohol is banned in Somalia. As I landed in Mogadishu and arrived at the inspectors, I wondered why I had ever agreed to bring tequila to a conservative Muslim country, but I made it through undetected.

I had arranged to stay at a place called Peace Hotel, where aid workers, foreign correspondents, and other Western visitors liked to put themselves up. A concierge of sorts from the hotel met me at arrivals and ushered me outside into a dense heat that slathered my skin. He walked me to the parking lot, past a checkpoint where a security guard was only letting in people with passports and tickets, to another man who guided me into an armored black sport utility vehicle and then climbed into the driver's seat. The door was so heavy it took several tries for me to close it. We drove out of the airport, through more checkpoints manned by Ugandan soldiers who looked bored and wary, and then by the Green Zone, where the United Nations, foreign embassies, and African Union peacekeepers all shared a fortified base. After a few moments, we reached the hotel. When I asked the receptionist why I needed an armored car for the short ride from the airport, she told me with delight that it would withstand bomb blasts: "You will just bounce!"

I had come to Mogadishu to meet the girls playing basketball despite the threats to their lives. I had seen a photo essay of some of the players a few years earlier, and thought they were some of the bravest people I had ever heard of. It was both an ordinary and rare kind of bravery, the kind that they didn't think about every day because they were just trying to live their lives, but that was incredible considering the danger they faced.

Aisha was now seventeen. When we first met at a game, I was talking to a group of giggly players in the bleachers, and she came and sat next to us. Without much prompting, Aisha immediately began telling me about some of her perilous encounters. Beautiful and outspoken, her face was endearingly expressive. She had a tiny gold nose ring that it took a few long looks at her to notice. She liked to talk, a lot, in her scratchy, high voice while gesturing with her hands. Aisha occasionally stopped to think for a moment by breathing out a "hmm" or "haa," and then kept talking for as long as she could. At practice, her coach made her do push-ups when she didn't stop talking. She had a compulsive need to be honest about what she thought and felt. When she asked me if I was dating anyone, and I said I wasn't, she said matter-of-factly to her friend in Somali, "She's the same age as my mother."

One morning a couple of weeks after we met, Aisha invited me to her half sister's home. She was wearing a hot pink jilbab, a head covering that swept around her face and down past her waist, with a long yellow skirt in a blue floral design. She wore wedged sandals. When she sat down, though, I noticed black track pants peeking from under the bottom of her skirt. "I usually wear them," she said, grinning. I observed that she seemed somewhat small for basketball. "Yeah, I'm short, but there are a lot of players who are short and really good," she said. "The playing should be from your heart and not dependent on how tall you are." She had a game that night, and she promised that she would point out a girl who was tall, but who didn't know how to shoot.

Basketball was just one of Aisha's duties. Every morning, she cleaned, did laundry, and cooked breakfast for herself, her mother, and her younger brother. She prepared lahoh, savory crepes rolled with butter, sugar, or honey. Sometimes they had goat or camel kidney meat with bread, a traditional breakfast meal, or fried eggs. It was the family's time to catch up and check in with each other. Aisha did most of the cooking, but if she wasn't around, they had a house cleaner who would fill in. She also attended a technical school, not far from her house, where she was taking computer classes a few times a week. When she had practice, she would get dressed in her athletic clothes underneath her jilbab, blouse, and skirt and head to the court to work out in the tiny exercise room or practice her shooting. She usually practiced twice a day, six days a week. Occasionally, they had games. Friday, the holy day of the week, was her day off.

Life could be like that, pleasant and straightforward, until it wasn't. One afternoon in late April, her older brother Abdi left his university in Mogadishu after classes ended and began to make his way home. It was a hot, bright day, the kind that squeezed you tired. Abdi had stopped in a pharmacy to buy medicine for their mother, who had diabetes. Two men were arguing nearby and they shot at each other. Her brother was hit by one of the bullets. The men lived, and her brother died. "He was happy, he loved me," Aisha said. "He supported me and stood up for me in the family." Abdi understood Aisha, her moods and her temperament, and he was often the peacemaker of the family. He had wanted to be an engineer. He was friendly to everyone he met, and Aisha was the closest to him of all her siblings. He was only twenty-two.

Abdi's death reminded Aisha that life in her country could be short and cruel, ending with a shock of violence and then fading into nothing. So many of her friends and teammates had left to illegally immigrate to Europe through Libya. "I want to leave this country," she said. "Because it's not safe here. Anything can happen to you." When I told her how sorry I was to hear of her brother's death, she slightly bowed her head and lifted her shoulders. "This is the life," she said. "No one stays alive forever."

PART TWO

1

UGANDA

In a Perfect Life

AFTER EUNICE escaped, Bosco didn't hear from her, or hear news of her, for three months. Then, one day, as Bosco was talking with another rebel, a familiar voice came on the radio. It was Eunice. She was safe in Gulu with their son.

After a fitful night of sleep in the forest, Eunice and Edimon had come upon people working in a garden, and she asked for their help. They put her in a vehicle that dropped her off at the army barracks in Gulu. After announcing her arrival on the radio, Eunice had gone to a rehabilitation center, one of several run by nonprofits that helped former combatants get back on their feet.

LRA commanders realized that Eunice was missing from the camp through her radio message. Because the rebels roamed in far-flung groups to avoid detection, none of the leaders had noticed Eunice's disappearance yet. When they asked Bosco how she had fled, he told them that she had wandered out of his sight during battle and been rescued by the army. They believed him. Eunice was dead, his commanders told him, and her voice was just a recording. Bosco wondered if they were telling the truth. "I was not going to escape if I didn't think she was alive," he recalled. He had no access to outside information—the rebels had been his schooling and his source of news for years, and Kony said his words came from God—and so Bosco had no choice but to accept what they said. Why risk trying to escape if his family was already dead? If the rebels didn't kill him, the military would.

About a year later, Bosco was sent on patrol from the LRA's base in Sudan with a few other men. Along the route, he stopped two boys he recognized from his home area to ask if his mother was alive, and if Eunice had returned. The boys said yes. (His father, however, had been shot and killed by the LRA.) Bosco was elated and ready to do anything to reach home. When he was unable to persuade the rebels with him to escape, he shot them. He then loitered in the bush for two weeks until he thought it was safe to surrender.

He ended up at Gulu's military base, full of soldiers who had once hunted him and who were now sleeping, eating, and hanging out, and he was told they wanted to transfer him to a rehabilitation center. Instead, he left the base to go find his family. "With the love I had for my mother and Eunice, I couldn't stay in the barracks," Bosco said. Eunice had heard that her mother, Margaret, was alive and went to see her after a few weeks of therapy and sewing training at her rehabilitation center. She went back home and found her mother sick, but overjoyed to see her and her grandson. Margaret had thought that she would never see her daughter again. Eunice, who had become a graceful young woman, was going to give birth to her second child, and was relieved to be in a place where she could bring up children and give them things she had not experienced in a long time: real meals, space to play and be free, school, safety.

Bosco's mother, Auma, had also heard Eunice on the radio. She had listened in shock when Eunice said that she had returned with the child of a rebel named Bosco. She came to find Eunice at her mother's home. "She asked me, 'Is my son really alive?'" Eunice recalled. "I told her that he would try to follow me, and she asked if I was sure that I would wait for him. I told her I would. I had his children, and I believed he was coming. I did ask myself, if I had not had a child with him, would I still wait? But I couldn't imagine being with someone who had not faced the same conditions in the bush. I thought it would be so hard to be with someone who doesn't know what I'm experiencing; I was having nightmares. I needed someone who understood what I had been through, and I was praying that he would come back and that we would be together." In early 2005, Bosco made it home from the base to see Auma. Then, nervous and excited, he set off for Eunice's mother's house without telling anyone there he was coming. He showed up at the compound and came face-to-face with Eunice. She dropped what she was holding and stared at him in shock. Eunice tried to lift Bosco, and then he tried to carry her, and they both collapsed into each other, laughing and crying.

Bosco told Eunice's mother that they had been in the bush together. He asked her if she would allow Eunice to join him in his village so that they could live as a couple. Margaret refused. Eunice's other relatives, who were upset that Eunice wanted to reunite with Bosco, also refused. Margaret told Bosco that he had abducted her daughter and forced her to be his wife. She blamed him for all the misery Eunice had endured since she was taken. Eunice pleaded with her mother, and Margaret seemed to soften. If Bosco paid a dowry, she said, she would allow a marriage. In Acholi culture, men were required to pay dowries to the families of their intended wives; Margaret knew Bosco could not pay. He had neither money nor animals. Eunice was furious.

In a fit of rage and frustration she still could not understand, she ingested poison and set fire to her hut on her family compound. Her family stopped her before she burned the whole place down. They rushed her to the hospital. "I wanted to do a lot of damage and then kill myself. I was so happy to see him, and had been afraid that he would not come back. I thought of him most of the time, particularly when the children were sick and I needed his help and comfort," Eunice told me. If she couldn't be with Bosco, she would have to find a new partner from her community, a man she knew would insult and abuse her because of her past. She began her adult life with Bosco. She had children with him. This was the way things were supposed to be. Eunice was desperate. The prospect of losing him again was too frightening. The next day, her mother relented and let them leave together. "She said, 'To hell with them,'" Bosco remembered.

Eunice's mother was not the only parent who viewed couples like Eunice and Bosco as illegitimate. Across the north, families watched with dismay as their daughters reunited with the men to whom they were assigned in the bush. Santo Lazech, an official at Ker Kal Kwaro Acholi, or the Acholi Cultural Institution, told me that the unions were "disheartening." The cultural institution was a kind of judicial and governing body for the Acholis that ruled according to tradition, unlike Uganda's formal legal system. I went to see him early one morning before people began filtering into his office to ask his guidance on a variety of family matters and legal disputes. He was an agreeable man with a round belly and a patient disposition. "They defeat my understanding of family and love. Do the women not reflect back on the time of abduction?" Lazech went on. "What about their feelings of humiliation and oppression?"

Evelyn Lapat used to be a counselor at a rehabilitation center that aided young mothers who had returned with their children. Lapat was in her thirties and, like a great number of women in the region, had been abducted— briefly, for three months in 1997. It took some searching to find her. Six years after the war in Uganda had ended, most of the rehabilitation centers in Gulu had closed their counseling programs, and I couldn't find any therapists who had worked with female returnees. After leaving one rehabilitation center, which now stood lifeless except for a few staff, I hailed a *boda boda*, a motorbike taxi, to my hotel. During the ride, the driver turned halfway toward me and asked if I worked at the center. He was wearing a bomber jacket and sunglasses, and he was young and handsome. He told me, with a smile, that he had stayed at the center when he first came back from the bush. I hoped he was managing to build a life for himself, wherever he was living.

When I did track down Lapat, through her former colleagues, and we met in the grassy backyard of a popular restaurant, she asked me not to mention the name of the organization where she had worked and she glanced around at the other diners, looking to see if she knew anyone. "Some of the women decided to go back to men who had once beat and raped them," Lapat told me. When the women returned from the bush, the men's families would find them at the center and offer to take care of them and their children. If the women's own families were living in refugee camps, the offers were attractive. Many of the women were from the countryside and had not gone through much schooling before abduction, and their employment prospects were bleak. The women who trained as tailors set up shop in markets only to find no business. Customers whispered that they were *dwogo cen paco* ("come back home") and avoided their tables. Even if the women's families could house them, they often didn't want their children. With rebels as fathers, the children were supposedly cursed with toxic spirits.

The prime minister of the Acholi Cultural Institution, then a stately man named Kenneth Oketta, told me he had seen numerous instances where women sought out their bush husbands who had joined the army after escaping the LRA. But when the women found them at the barracks, the men pretended not to know them and refused to take responsibility for their children. The men said they wanted new lives. "These single mothers without family support are traumatized. They have to rent somewhere in town or live like a refugee. Survival here means access to land, which is family land," Oketta said. Women were expected to live and raise children in the homes of their husbands' families. If the women did find new partners, Oketta saw the husbands turn on their wives in times of financial or marital strife, accusing them of causing their misfortune by bringing back evil from the bush.

"He has wasted me," one woman told Lapat. Another woman asked her, "When our children grow up, they will want to know their father, so why not go back to him now? What can I do?" For the most part, they went back to their bush husbands not out of love, but because they felt ruined and believed no other man would love them and their children. The women's psychological dependence on the men became entangled with the importance of clans in Acholi culture. When a couple had children, the man's clan then became responsible for the care of the woman and the children. "They may not be happy or in love, but they have clear consciences that they are taking care of their children," Lapat said. And because

Acholis view marriage as a symbol of honor and respect
for women, much like many Americans do, and arranged
marriages were performed as recently as Lapat's mother's
generation, young mothers who had returned told me
they felt satisfaction in at least having a partner to provide for their needs. Suddenly being on her own could be
confusing to a woman once in the bush, and could make
her feel hopeless. During the 2008 peace negotiations between the LRA and the government, one of Kony's wives,
who had been rescued and returned to Gulu, attempted
to cross back into southern Sudan to rejoin the warlord.
Authorities apprehended her before she reached her destination.

Ida, a soft-spoken woman in her early thirties with
a youthful beauty, was forced to be with a commander
when she was fourteen. She had two children while in
captivity. I found her through the Refugee Law Project,
a Ugandan organization preserving the stories of war
survivors, most of whom suffered from untreated post-
traumatic stress disorder. After the commander let Ida
escape in 2004, she settled in Gulu. She had few fond
memories of her bush husband, Michael. He was abusive
and tempestuous. But when he returned a year later and
she heard his voice on the radio, she rushed to see him.
She hoped he had changed and would take care of her
and their children. Now she lived with him and said that
they had begun to understand each other, a step away
from the fear and hate she felt for him for most of their
time together in the bush. At one point Ida told me that
she loved him. I tried to believe her, but couldn't. Later

she admitted, "I cannot say anything about love because I don't know the meaning of love." The two did seem like they had reached a mutual understanding and were trying to live together the best they could, but I wouldn't have called her happy. Michael, who wore a patch over an eye he lost in battle, still seemed severe and authoritative. When they sat on their couch, in a simple hut in a Gulu shantytown, he sat at one end and she perched at the other. It was impossible to look at Ida and not imagine the other lives she could have led, and wish she had lived them.

Michael had several wives while in the bush, and another ex-partner, Jacqueline, also resided in Gulu. She had spiky hair dyed blond and big white teeth; I found her in a tiny hair salon that had a few chairs and mirrors, a television, and a stereo. She was working as a stylist. Photographs of women in somewhat outdated hairstyles decorated the purple walls. When I showed up one July afternoon in 2012, she told me, "I've told him not to come where I am, and that he can't see my child. When I see him on the road, I refuse to greet him. I was so young and he treated me so badly." She was now with a different man, though it took me a while to realize the child she had with Michael lived with her grandmother. She wasn't very forthcoming about the whereabouts of her boy. Her parents and new partner refused to accept the son of a rebel.

Yet there can be bonds within these couples that are hard to explain. Pamela Anena, a thirty-year-old willowy singer who was abducted at the age of thirteen and forced

to be the partner of one of Kony's bodyguards for the almost two years she spent in captivity, said the feelings she
had for him were complicated. While she resented him
for spoiling her childhood, she empathized with his emotional and moral struggles. After she escaped and made it
to a rehabilitation center, his family made regular visits to
see her even though she had no children with him. The
bodyguard eventually died in battle, but Anena told me,
"I would have considered being with him if he had come
to my home to ask my parents." We didn't talk about the
question I hadn't asked, but that hovered uneasily in the
air: Would she ever get a second chance with someone
else?

After reuniting, Eunice and Bosco lived in a refugee camp
for a few months, before moving into a modest hut of
their own on Bosco's family compound in 2007. To Eunice and Bosco's surprise, Eunice's mother offered an
apology, and the couple forgave her. The day Eunice,
Bosco, and I first met, in July of 2012, we sat outside
in their courtyard on small wooden chairs. Heavy clouds
floated above us; it was the height of the rainy season.
As we talked, Eunice and Bosco told me how much they
reveled in the tranquility of the place. Both farmers, they
worked in the green fields in the early mornings; Eunice
cooked for the family; they both shopped and socialized
at the local market and went to church on Sundays; and
they played with their children, two daughters and one
son. The family was poor. They had to save up to afford
meat for their meals, and the children were out of school

when I saw them again in 2014 because their fees hadn't been paid—they had a new toddler then, a son named Tadeo, after the Slovenian photographer Tadej I first traveled with to meet the couple. But, as Eunice told me, she and Bosco were "living together like people who were not forced to be together." Without the stain of the bush.

But Bosco, who had grown into a quiet man with long limbs, high cheekbones, and an easy smile, drank with an alarming frequency when he first returned. Life had been hard in the camp, and was even more difficult when they returned to his family's land. In the bush, if you needed food or medicine, you could just loot it. Here, the farming was grueling, and Bosco suffered from severe stomach and chest pains: leftover aches from the work he did while in captivity. Then there were the challenges of feeding his children; Eunice had given birth to their second child.

The bush forced many things upon him: family, responsibility for the life and death of others before he was ready or knew what to do with it. It also took things away: the chance to continue his education, the hope of any kind of real prosperity away from the rural life he had always known. And then there were the things people said. When Eunice went to fetch water, people would gossip that she was the one who had returned, only to go back to her bush husband. Some people were happy and relieved that she had returned, but others feared her. They would visit her and leave quickly. When speaking about that time to me, she became upset, fighting back tears. Bosco's stepmother told Eunice's sister-in-law that Eunice should not be living with them since she had a rebel mind, a backward mentality. "I was hurt," Eunice said. "I did not tell her that I was angry. I just left it. But I was really hurt." I could see the pain in her face, which she turned away from me.

Bosco experienced something similar. "When I first came back, some of the neighbors said behind my back that I've come back from the bush, yet I have killed a lot of people. They said the government of Uganda is very stupid; instead of killing me, they rescued me," Bosco recalled. "The good thing is that I was born and grew up here, so some people sympathized with me." He still faced hostile neighbors, but his relatives were the ones who lived in his immediate surroundings, a peaceful, expansive compound. Also, others came to him to express appreciation and gratitude because he had freed them in the bush after the LRA had kidnapped them, and then directed them to safety.

Still, in the first years after their escape, his pain brought on anger. Eunice assumed that he was drinking out of frustration with their son Edimon. The little boy was having seizurelike spells. Bosco became aggressive and would bark orders at Eunice, behavior that reminded her of being in captivity. "I was not happy either, but he chose to drink," Eunice said. She cried as we talked.

Eunice could surprise you with her loveliness. One day, she wore a pale pink billowing blouse made of light cotton and a purple checkered headscarf; she glowed, and the angles of her face were delicate and striking. In those moments, it was difficult to imagine her life of captivity. "It hurt me so much," she said of Bosco's behavior. After four unhappy years, Bosco's relatives intervened, pressuring him to cut back on his drinking. He started receiving counseling from a local organization and carpentry training from another. Eunice, meanwhile, tried to keep the past at bay. Her way of making the most of the present was to not think about the pains of her abduction and the bush, and to push those memories down when they surged forward. She needed to quell her doubts about Bosco; she knew that, deep down, he was good. Nearly all the women she knew from the LRA who had escaped were with their rebel husbands. "I wanted to be with him, to be happy in our marriage," she told me. She had made up her mind early on. "I always wanted to be with just one man." She was sometimes reasoning with herself: "He took care of me when I was in the bush. That's why I came back safely."

Discrimination against them was pervasive. It was not easy to join community groups, and neighbors complained that they brought back evil when their son became sick. Both wished they had undergone a proper reconciliation ceremony, an elder-guided ritual called *mato oput* that brought victims and perpetrators together in a process of confession, compensation, and forgiveness. At the end, they drank a bitter herb from the same gourd with the vow, "Let's all drink from this bitterness so that we do not get into this again," Oketta told me. They believed a cleansing ceremony would have been enough to rid them of the spirits they killed, but the process was too expensive for them. They needed money and animals they didn't have.

Several people had stopped Bosco over the years since he had returned, and asked if he was the one who killed the son, or daughter, or brother, or other relative of a community member. "People confronted me and said I had beaten or killed their relatives, but that could even be my first time meeting them; I didn't know them. I told them it was not me. I'm from here and could not kill anyone from the same place. But I could tell from their moods that they did not believe me," Bosco recalled. When they wouldn't stop asking him, Bosco pretended that he had to make a phone call and then got away. Perhaps, he admitted to me, when he was young and first abducted, he could have killed residents from around there, but he did not remember.

In a place where every family had been affected by the war, it was not simply a matter of victims versus perpetrators. Nearly everyone recognized that the perpetrators were also victims. The tension lay in the hurt, anger, and jealousy over loved ones murdered or missing in light of the abducted ones who came back, and in a growing desire to blame grievances on someone. On my trip in 2012, my interpreter Victor Oloya and I began asking around Eunice and Bosco's village for parents of children who had been abducted by the LRA, but who had not escaped. Victor himself had been abducted as a boy, and spent several years in the bush. Toweringly tall, with big, kind eyes, he now worked as an interpreter, a fixer, a researcher, and a consultant for various nongovernmental organizations. He counseled others who had broke free from the bush, and struck me as one of the most sensitive people I had ever met.

We were led to Christine Ajok, a sixty-five-year-old widow who lived a few miles down the road from Bosco and Eunice, and who agonized daily over the whereabouts of her son. "I don't know if he's alive or dead and it's been so long. People are now coming back, but I still don't see him," Ajok told me. None of the returnees had told her any information about him, and while she thought it was good fortune that they had returned, she was angry that her son had not come back, too. She was not well. She rambled incoherently at times and lost focus during our conversation. Her neighbors said she was going mad because of her loss.

Oketta, the Acholi prime minister, had observed Acholis shift from offering forgiveness to needing justice. "People feel wronged, and now they want redress," he said. Some harassed returnees with threats of revenge or even legal challenges. Land disputes, domestic violence, and other conflicts simmered between returnees and those who remained behind. Survivors of the war were economically disadvantaged and felt ignored by their government. The returned fighters served as daily reminders of people's frustration with the lack of accountability for what had happened to them, and the ex-rebels were often tormented by their communities.

The government ended blanket amnesty in 2012, making the status of LRA fighters who recently returned unclear. An official at the Amnesty Commission, which provided 5,000 LRA returnees with resettlement packages of money, seeds, farm tools, and bedding and helped them move back home, told me that when LRA soldiers in the bush learned of the end of amnesty, they would simply stop returning and feel compelled to fight to the death. If any returnees did end up at the commission, the agency had orders to turn them over to the Directorate of Public Prosecutions.

The Amnesty Act was created because of a grassroots movement to put an end to twenty-odd rebellions boiling in the late 1990s, and government officials conceded that amnesty had been crucial in establishing the peace that had settled over northern Uganda. But now the international community had interpreted blanket amnesty as letting criminals go unpunished, another amnesty commission official observed. In order not to jeopardize its aid funds, Uganda quickly fell in line and dropped its amnesty policy. In 2008, the government set up a war crimes court with funding from donor countries and support from foreign human rights organizations. Since then, Uganda had only had one case before the court, and government officials told me that their Western partners were getting antsy. The pending case of an LRA commander named Thomas Kwoyelo, who was abducted as a child, put the government in the awkward position of arguing that its own amnesty legislation was unconstitutional when Kwoyelo surrendered. At the end of 2016, his trial still hadn't begun.

When Victor and I first visited Eunice and Bosco in the summer of 2012, their son Edimon later asked Eunice why we were there. The twelve-year-old was curious about the stranger asking his parents so many questions. Eunice told him as little as she could: that she and his father had been in the bush with the LRA, and that I was there to support them. Despite our best attempts to shoo the children away, Edimon overheard some of what his parents told me about their lives in the bush. Two years later, a radio show advertised a scholarship program for children born into captivity. Eunice was excited and told Edimon she wanted him to apply, and immediately his sickness, the shaking spells he had had since he was a young boy, worsened. They never went to the radio station. I wondered: Did she blame me for Edimon now knowing what she had tried to hide from him? She had wanted to protect him. Even if she didn't, I blamed myself.

Beginning when he was seven, Edimon's spells or seizures initially lasted for only a few minutes. Then he would be alert again. Now, for one to two hours he was practically comatose, as if he were not breathing. Before he fell into a fit, Edimon would beg his mother to help him, tell her to pour water on him, and then it would seem as if all the energy had drained from his body. Edimon had no memory of doing any of this. Eunice held the baby, Tadeo, close to her as she relived the possessions. Tadeo was coughing and fidgeting, but Eunice seemed to be somewhere else. Why had Edimon's illness worsened after Eunice encouraged him to apply for the scholarship for children like him? It was evident that Eunice and Bosco were deeply traumatized from their abductions and

ensuing lives in the bush. My interviewing them wasn't
helping them forget their trauma. I tried to talk to both
of them with as much sensitivity as I could and express to
them how wrong and awful I felt their experiences had
been, but I was still asking them to recount horror and
pain. Had they passed their trauma on to their son? Was
that even possible?

Studies had found the rate of mental illness in northern
Uganda to be one of the highest in the world, with one
study counting over half of adults in two northern districts,
including Gulu, as suffering from PTSD. Few mental
health clinics existed in the region, so people struggled
to treat anxiety, paranoia, and depression. Some coped
through heavy drinking and drug use. Everyone was un-
well: those who were abducted and raped; those who had
their relatives die in brutal, unimaginable ways; those who
had their body parts cut off for fun by rebels; and those
who saw it all happen. No one was spared. I read about one
ten-year-old boy kept in the mental ward of a Gulu hospital six years earlier, screaming from visions even though he
was too young to remember much of the war.

When I visited the family again in 2014, they told me
that Edimon's fits were getting worse. Eunice and Bosco
believed Edimon was possessed. Bosco told me the possession had come about because he had killed people,
and those murders had infected his son with what are
called *cen*, or bad spirits, in Acholi. "We consulted with
the Acholi cultural institution. They said that for Edimon
to survive, the cleansing ceremony needs to be done be-

cause the spirits of the people I killed are still waiting. Otherwise my son will die and the spirits will move to another child until all my children are dead," he said. Bosco's mother sought out a spiritual healer who said the same. The ceremony would cost $150, one sheep, and two goats. When Bosco later asked me for a donation, he did so in English, and hearing him speak was like adjusting to seeing in the dark. I looked at him blankly for a few seconds. I hadn't realized his English was good enough to hold a basic conversation. "I am not happy about what is happening to my son," he told me. "I regret a lot. That the LRA abducted me and forced me to kill. I wish I had not had my son. I wish the LRA would have killed me in the bush.

"When they took me, I was young. I didn't know the difference between right and wrong," Bosco went on. As we talked, he was bent over from stomach pains on the floor of his home's sitting room, thinner than I had ever seen him.

Eunice tried to explain what Bosco meant when he talked about possession. "When we take Edimon to the hospital, they don't find anything," she said. "Bosco was forced to kill. I was also forced to kill. Maybe it's a combination of those people we killed, revenging on Edimon." She said that during Edimon's spells, he would say things like, "Why have you killed me?" or "Why have you shot me?" And, "You thought that I could not find you." Then he would become silent, drifting into a catatonic state. But where did those statements come from? I thought Eunice hadn't really killed anyone. Was the possession

Bosco's fault? She said she had killed two people. "I feel guilty and sometimes I ask for forgiveness," Eunice said. "I did this, but I did not want to do it." The rebels had beat the victims nearly to death, and then told her to finish them off. She and Victor commiserated over having to complete this type of killing, which made them murderers even though other people had done most of the work, and they started to laugh. They couldn't stop laughing. I was taken aback; it was a little disturbing, but somehow I understood.

Still, I hadn't believed in possessions since I was a kid in Sunday school. I needed to see Edimon. I thought that Eunice and Bosco had to be mistaken, that they were projecting their own nightmares and worries onto their innocent son.

They had sent him to a pastor who would attempt to expunge the *cen* from him. Eunice and Bosco had become born-again Christians, and they had faith in the powers of the church. Neighbors had donated money for Edimon's transportation to this miracle center. Victor and I drove thirty miles on his motorbike to the pastor's compound, where a house and church stood side by side near a trading center on a rural road. The pastor was named Innocent Okello, and turned out to be married to Bosco's niece. It was raining when we arrived, and Okello led Victor and me into the church, a low, spacious hut with a thatched roof. It was dim inside, and the only sound we heard was the rain. Okello was thin, with haunted eyes. As he described the nature of Edimon's possession, the dying and coming back to life, I wondered if what he said was true.

Edimon appeared; he was shy and tiny for fourteen, with wide eyes and a high voice. He was wearing a stained white button-down shirt. He said he was feeling okay, but that he didn't know what was happening to him or when it was going to happen, nor did he remember what had happened when it was over.

Before the possession, Edimon liked playing games and sports and doing traditional dances, and he was a talented drummer. He swept their home every Saturday and helped with the farming. He was a good boy. Everyone I talked to about him said the same thing: "God should help him."

Three times the family prepared to dig graves for Edimon. But he rose up the first time, then again the second and third times, reviving from whatever hold the spirits had on him. For a while, he was paralyzed, unable to walk or move properly. Their neighbors came to discuss what to do about Edimon. Someone suggested he be taken to Okello.

Edimon didn't make eye contact with me. He looked straight ahead or down at the ground, squirming in his seat the whole time as if he wanted to flee, his short legs swinging back and forth. As the pastor looked on, Edimon said he didn't know anything about his parents' abductions. I asked him what he thought caused his fits. Maybe, he answered, because of the atrocities his parents committed in the bush. I stopped. But how he did know about any violence? He said he was guessing, but no one had told him. I gently asked him again. When I first visited Eunice and Bosco two years ago, he finally said, he had overheard some things they told me. It wasn't unusual that his parents had not told him any details about their past; parents who came back usually wanted to avoid talking about their time in captivity because of the stigma attached to their abductions. Edimon began crying. We walked him back outside, and Victor and I hugged him before leaving. We told him everything would be all right. His father was visiting soon. He looked forlorn, too fragile to exist in this place.

Eunice and Bosco believed that the preacher could only chase the spirits away temporarily. Neighbors had taken pity on the family, and their compound was suddenly full of visitors inquiring about the health of their son and advising Eunice and Bosco to raise funds for a cleansing ceremony. Bosco was tortured over his responsibility for what was happening to Edimon. He killed people because he did not want to be killed. "I still cannot believe that I am accountable for it," he said. But it was difficult to make peace with it.

In history, there were the choices people made and the choices made for them, and then there was the murky in-between. What was happening to Edimon? I decided to look more closely at the idea of intergenerational trauma. It was now widely believed that some wives and even children of American soldiers returning from duty in Iraq and Afghanistan were suffering from what was called secondary trauma—symptoms like depression, acute stress, and paranoia absorbed from soldiers in the throes of PTSD. The experience of families sharing trauma after one or more members go through violent experiences was not new. It dated back to the Vietnam War. Robert Motta, a clinical psychologist who studied secondary trauma in the families of Vietnam veterans, once said that trauma was "contagious." It could affect anyone who was in close, sustained contact with it. It could, more or less, possess them.

Traditional war didn't seem to be the right comparison to the captivity Eunice and Bosco had endured. More comparable, perhaps, was Hiroshima, when the United States dropped two atomic bombs on two Japanese cities during World War II. After the bombings, the survivors who were exposed to radiation were known as *hibakusha*, meaning explosion-affected people, and the name carried significant stigma. Hibakusha hid their experiences from neighbors and colleagues, and their relatives did the same because they knew others would perceive them as being spoiled. The families of hibakusha began to share their conditions—nightmares, paranoia—and, in some cases, it was almost as if the relative of a hibakusha had been there during the bombing, too. Children, even grandchildren, were shaken by an event they had not known intimately. They had only heard stories about the bombs, and re-alized those stories were the reason why the hibakusha in their lives had always been off, perpetually disturbed, never quite there. The amount of unexpected devastation a person who lived through an atomic blast would feel seemed similar to what a child would experience after be-ing forcibly conscripted by a savage rebel group. The howl of suffering and loss from the victims of the LRA bore re-semblance.

Edimon was back home within a few months and going to school again. But his possession was still ongoing.

I came to believe that Edimon's condition was a case of
transgenerational trauma. It seemed the only reasonable
cause for his frightening recitation of words Bosco recalled his victims saying to him before he killed them,
pleas for mercy. And words he thought they would say to
him now, vows of revenge for their deaths. Later, other
medical explanations would occur to me, like psychoso-
matic disorders. But I believed then that it was transgenerational trauma because I could see how I had also become
possessed by Eunice and Bosco's stories. After my first visit
with them in the summer of 2012, I returned to New
York feeling unmoored and not knowing why. Every day
for several weeks, I listened to my audio recordings of our
interviews, transcribing and writing notes. I then spent
more weeks writing. All the while, I felt listless, sleepless,
like I had stumbled into a dark place from which I could
not emerge—what a doctor would later identify as symptoms of depression.

I was obsessed, too. I thought about Eunice and Bosco
constantly, talked about them with friends and relatives.
People would tell me that it was such an unusual experience that I had in northern Uganda, and that it must have
been really sad. It had been sad, but that was only part
of why the story had consumed me. I had conducted an
extensive, invasive procedure on Eunice and Bosco, pried
into their lives and had them tell me their most personal
thoughts and encounters. The end result was sometimes

unsettling, sometimes surprisingly familiar. I had become part of their lives, and they were now part of mine. I wondered about the parts of them I didn't know.

When I returned to northern Uganda two years later, I was no longer feeling depressed, but I was still fixated on Eunice and Bosco. I felt a fondness and deep respect for Eunice. When I reported in Africa, I tended to think along the lines of an old maxim: *There but for the grace of God go I.* I was also once an African girl, like Eunice. And, but for the grace of fate, I could have been born outside of Gulu instead of the sprawling, hot state of Texas. I lived in the Ugandan capital city Kampala for two years right out of college, in a sliver of a country that wasn't even bigger than the state where I was born. Ugandans assumed I was one of them until I opened my mouth to speak, and I reveled in being able to blend in and move around mostly unnoticed.

My parents understood that feeling well, and they longed for it when they found themselves foreigners in a new land. They were the only Nigerians in the library hall one autumn day at Alabama State University. It was the 1970s, and both had come, within a few years of each other, to a state so far south that the tip of it hangs precariously into the Gulf of Mexico. It was a place full of green fields with cattle; small towns with not much more than churches, liquor stores, and fast-food restaurants; and slightly more cosmopolitan cities like the one where they lived, Montgomery. Naturally, they were drawn to each other. The way my mother told the story, my dad spotted her studying across the library at a long wooden table and wouldn't stop staring in her direction. He was work-ing a part-time job at the circulation desk. Disturbed, my mother turned away from my father, who was gazing at her without so much as a blink. She eventually relaxed when he came over and introduced himself. My mom was vivacious and outspoken. My dad was brooding and in-tense and fell for her quickly.

My parents had something else important in common other than their nationality. They were both attending college in the Deep South at the tail end of the Civil Rights Movement. My mom, who I often think would make a great soap opera actress, loved to retell the scenes of how they met and later became close: lonely winter breaks when my dad invited her and her sister to stay with him in his apartment because they couldn't afford the ex-pensive trip home to Nigeria; summer dates spent explor-ing the sleepy town of Montgomery; meals of spicy *jollof* rice and pepper soup that she cooked and that they shared at his place. As my parents married and moved through the region—Texas, Tennessee, and Alabama again—they shared the triumphs and disappointments and the unique strangeness that came with being black and African in the South.

Both of my parents endured bigoted classmates and professors and the racial tension that crackled in most places then. Not long after my then-twentysomething Nigerian father transferred to Alabama State University, a historically black school in downtown Montgomery, he saw the Ku Klux Klan marching in the streets. Still, those things were minor obstacles to living the American immigrant's dream. My father, who grew up poor in the frenetic, coarse megacity of Lagos, became a journalism professor. My mother, who grew up in a wealthier family in a small village, worked as a nurse and then a professor of nursing. This was the reason, they both thought, that they left their family and friends so many miles away in what had become so many years ago.

"As soon as I retire, we are going back to Nigeria— we are already building a house there," my dad told me throughout my childhood, sometimes showing me photos of a house in the early stages of construction. Moving back to Nigeria was always the fuzzy plan they had since they emigrated. Move to America, go to a good university, and then go back home to build a life. But the definition of "home" itself became confusing. There was the place where they first played with their brothers and sisters and sneaked out to parties. And there was the place where they became adults and dual citizens. The political and security situation in Nigeria worsened. When they occasionally visited, their homecomings increasingly felt like visiting a foreign country. And so, as children, my brothers and I had Nigerian nostalgia around us, all the time.

My parents belonged to an association made up of the Africans who lived in our town. Ghanaians, Liberians, and Nigerians would gather during the summer and holidays for parties over platters of food and in tune to rousing West African music, and our laughter could be heard several banquet halls away because we were happy, and because West Africans were notoriously loud. We couldn't help it. The room was a kaleidoscope of color from the stiff ankara fabric the women wore in a stunning array of pinks, purples, yellows, and blues. Following Nigerian custom, the men set off early in the morning to a nearby farm to kill, by hand, goats that were later roasted for the feast. The mental image of my dad, along with the other African dads who were math professors, accountants, and doctors, running after goats in his tweed blazer never failed to horrify me.

When I told my parents that I wanted to move to Uganda to intern at a local newspaper after graduation, we sat at the kitchen table and tried to reason it out together. My mom was still resistant to the idea. I told them that I was a product of their deferred returns to Nigeria, and their constant yearning to be near family and compatriots. I told them that I wanted to experience my other home continent. They confessed that they were afraid. But their concerns—crime, instability, and lack of everyday luxuries—didn't seem like enough to keep me from going. I realized my desire to move was forcing my parents to confront, after decades, the reasons why they had left. And to perhaps regret never returning.

"It's just been such a long time," my dad said simply. Long since they had lived in Nigeria, long since they had known what it felt like to navigate the unpredictability and mundaneness of being in Africa. Still, we agreed that I should go and experience it for myself. I did, and it eventually led me to Eunice.

More than both having dark skin and being African, Eunice and I were both ordinary women: She loved, hated, craved, wondered, and contemplated as much as I did. She had found just herself in an extraordinary situation. I had no idea what choices I would have made had I been in her place, but I admired the resistance in the actions that had seemed the simplest to her. She returned home despite the LRA's attempt to rip her from all that she had known, despite its attempt to make her an unrecognizable soldier in its cultlike brigade. She then fought to be with a man against the extreme prejudice of her community. "You will not break me," she seemed to be saying with every decision she made. "Not again."

I had met Bosco's mother, Auma, several times. She lived near the couple, and was often at their home when I visited. She had expressed to me her relief at having her son and daughter-in-law home with her, and her unconditional acceptance of what they had to do in the bush. Eunice's mother, Margaret, wasn't as easygoing. When Victor and I went to see Margaret, at Eunice's childhood home, she was surprisingly spry despite her advanced age. She was petite and gentle, and had alert, bright eyes and a round face that was barely wrinkled. She was wearing a floral wrap skirt and a green blouse with white buttons. Her family compound reminded me of Bosco's, but was quieter and more spacious, less trees and high grass, with more bare ground. We entered a hut with her, and she curled up in a corner, humming and peeling nuts in a giant bowl.

I asked her how she felt when Eunice returned. "I

was very happy," Margaret recalled. "But then she started telling me what she did—or what she was forced to do—in the bush..." She trailed off. To make matters worse, Margaret felt, Eunice wanted to insult her mother's pain and return to Bosco. Though Margaret eventually relented, she still resented the marriage. To this day, she wanted to bring Eunice back to her proper home. Bosco wasn't taking care of her anyway, she thought—Eunice was too skinny and Edimon was sick.

"I felt bad because she was forced to do those things," she went on. "And it has now backfired," she said, referring to Edimon's possession. "I regret that she did those things, but it was also not her fault."

Toward the end of our conversation, when I pressed her to explain what was wrong about Eunice being with Bosco—did she believe he was a bad person?—Margaret lied to us. She said the couple had actually lived together before being abducted, and that Bosco's mother took their children in after they were taken. Later Eunice told me Margaret said this because she became afraid: Were we asking so many questions because we belonged to the Amnesty Commission and were looking for ex-rebels like Eunice and Bosco who had not yet publicly atoned for their sins? Their uncompleted cleansing ceremony hung over them like something menacing.

Her fears were not unfounded. Their government had little sympathy for the plight of people like them. President Museveni's spokesman, Tamale Mirundi, defended the government's new stance on amnesty to me. "What if these people are needed by the International Criminal

Court? They may be potential witnesses," he said. "Now that this is an international operation, we cannot let the hardcore criminals escape."

Even Oketta, the prime minister of the Acholi Cultural Institution, told me that amnesty was no longer as popular as it once was, now that people had to live with ex-fighters. Peace had been established, but there was need for community reconciliation, a truth-telling forum. "People could bring cases and say, 'Mr. So-and-So abducted her and up to now we have not seen her. Yet here he is walking free. Can he not tell us where she is?'" Oketta said. "But now everyone is left on their own, and feelings are smoldering." The government was supposedly trying to formalize traditional justice committees, but it was not clear if they would provide what northerners wanted: a policy that not only reconciled former rebels and survivors, but that also held Museveni's government and army accountable for the war.

Mapenduzi, the Gulu chairman, told me that the government should be mindful of the fact that so many children were still unaccounted for. His own younger brother was abducted and held for six years. "Amnesty is not about condoning impunity or protecting criminals," he said. "It's about finding a way to save those who have been kidnapped and leaving doors open." When the LRA was still active in Uganda and would come to towns for supplies, parents of abducted children felt conflicted about helping them. Some gave them food; they didn't want to think of their children going hungry. Mapenduzi was leaving soon for a trip to the Central African Republic with a nonprofit to teach locals that rebels escaping from the LRA deserved safe passage back to Uganda. Besides being killed by commanders if caught escaping, rebels were being killed by villagers in the Central African Republic, the Congo, and South Sudan who had suffered violence at the hands of the group. If they reached Uganda, the government put some former rebels into safe houses for long stays or forced them to work for the military as scouts, especially children. No kind of escape was easy.

For those who made it back, the daily tortures they faced were of a different kind. "I really want to be free, to move anywhere I want, but I'm very suspicious that if I have to go to the people I used to know, they will not be happy to see me," Bosco told me. "And I'm always suspicious that anything can happen to me." He instructed his children to come home immediately after classes ended at the primary school nearby. At seven in the evening, he called Eunice and their children together to eat at the fire they burned outside of their home. At nine, he required that everyone be inside the house before they then went to sleep. He and Eunice farmed in the mornings, and he limited his social interactions and errands to church and the trading center.

He could not stop thinking about a friend he had in the bush, another abducted boy. When his friend escaped, he first stayed in a refugee camp, where he was harassed because he had been forced to kill a person in their community. The relatives of the person he had killed had recognized him. He moved to a house behind the school with his wife and children, but the family would not leave him alone. One night a couple of years earlier, a group of people came and burned down his hut; his wife and children burned to death, and he was shot. Bosco used to have nightmares of people he killed. They would appear in his dreams and tell him that it was their turn to kill him now. He said prayer had helped make the nightmares go away. But he still worried people would take revenge on him.

Bosco had gone to only one counseling session since he returned. He wasn't sure therapy would help much, and he valued doing, taking care of his responsibilities, more than talking about the past. Edimon was still sick, but at least Bosco could watch over and protect him.

Eunice and Bosco took joy in the pleasures that they once never imagined experiencing. They sat at church and prayed together, spent time with their children in their clean, cozy home, and appreciated the hard-won tranquility they finally had. But Eunice secretly wanted them to leave and rent an apartment in town where people would not know anything about their background. "I don't know how we will all live together since the war has still not ended. If fighting resumes here, we could be identified as people who were once in the bush. And then what would happen to us?" she asked.

The couple thought that freedom would return to them the lives they once had; they had no idea of the mixed reception, and ultimately their own mixed feelings, that awaited them. "I wouldn't have chosen this for Eunice. But when I met her, I thought that having a wife and children would be the best thing," Bosco told me. Eunice wondered sometimes what life would have been like if she had not been taken. "In a perfect life, I would not be with Bosco," she said. "But I decided to give myself to him."

2

MAURITANIA

Caravan of Freedom

BY 8:00 P.M. on the night of the book burning, the backlash had begun. Local news websites posted articles calling Biram a heretic for setting on fire Islamic texts that endorsed slavery. Some editorials said he didn't even deserve a trial, that he should be put to death immediately. "When I went to bed, I was satisfied. It was the beginning of the change in the story of slavery in Mauritania. But I had a feeling something would happen tomorrow," Biram said. "When I woke up, it was a war—in the media, in the mosques." He was at peace with what he had done, and he prepared himself for the police.

As the hours dragged on without any sign of them, he thought the government must want him to escape, to run away, so that they wouldn't have to deal with him and the situation he had put them in. Why else had it not brought him into custody yet? His phone and Internet had stopped working. Activists flocked to his home, and a steady stream of press came for interviews. In the evening, some journalists told him they had seen police cars headed to his house. No one knew if the police would take him to jail or kill him, they said. They wanted to know his last words.

Biram told the reporters that he had accepted one of two things would happen: The state would kill him, and once it killed him, his death would spark a revolution among Haratin and lead to the decline of White Moor power. "So, in this case," he went on, "my death would be useful." If the state let him live, his survival would be a historic victory against White Moor power, and a new story would start. Behind his brave words, though, he was conflicted. He was uneasy about the idea of dying, but he didn't have a choice. So he steeled himself. Whatever happened next felt inevitable at this point. He fretted around his home, which was filling with supporters. "I was sure I would be killed because of this. I wasn't ready to die, but I was convinced it would happen. But for three years, I had wanted to do something that would really affect the lives of slaves in Mauritania," he said.

The irony was that, though he had burned books considered holy in Islam, Biram was a pious man. He never would have burned Islamic texts in any other circumstances. But those books deserved to be eradicated from the earth. He wouldn't listen to another person use them as the basis for why slavery was ordained by God, and that anger gave him the adrenaline to face his executioners. In front of the journalists he dared the state to kill him and set off riots.

The police came at nine thirty. They cut the electricity and raided his house in the dark as frightened neighbors watched from their windows and doorways. Biram was just as afraid, as he realized that his time had arrived. Policemen took him to their car, and three activists jumped into the vehicle with him. "It was dark and we didn't know where we were going," Biram recalled. They were brought to the police station and then separated. Biram's tiny cell was so filthy he couldn't lie down, and a swarm of mosquitoes kept him awake all night. At first, he had no idea what had happened to the activists who came to the jail with him. He was alone. But after the first night, the policemen briefly put him in another room with ten other IRA members they had also detained. Then they separated the activists again.

Policemen brought a television to his cell, and Biram watched Mauritanians campaigning for his death on the news. Thousands of people had gathered in the streets to protest against him. There were so many people the police couldn't contain them. He then watched President Aziz promise that he would punish Biram. But the policemen were strangely civil to him. The police chief came to his cell and asked him if he would explain on camera why he had burned the books. Biram refused when the policeman said they would not broadcast his explanation live; he knew they could manipulate the video. Politicians began to spread the rumor that he was an Israeli agent. "They said I work for the Jews," he recalled. "It's a way to make the Mauritanian people turn against me." The idea gained currency among White Moors. He was a terrorist, they told each other.

After two days in prison, the police allowed Leila to visit him. Policemen had been trying to search his home, but Biram's supporters had blocked access. Young male volunteers from the community, who called themselves a "peace committee," had been taking shifts protecting his body and his home. They had become his bodyguards. Biram believed, and it seemed to him other Haratin knew, that the movement was beginning to thrive with him at the head of it. White Moors were threatened by his activism, and he didn't know what lengths some would go to in order to stop him. "IRA cannot continue without me alive," he said. "Yet me being alive is dangerous to White Moors."

The police brought Leila to the prison in the hopes that Biram would convince her to let them fully search the house. After that, he didn't see her, his children, or anyone else from the outside world again. In the following weeks, Biram felt the most acute loneliness he had ever experienced in his life. The suffocating heat in his cell had taken a toll on his health. It didn't seem like he had anyone left on his side. The police were saying as much. "When they used the argument that we were fighting Islam, I had some doubts that IRA would survive this, that I would survive this," he said. He thought that if the propaganda continued and there was no urgent response to it, the movement would surely die. He felt regret for putting IRA members in danger.

But as soon as Biram had resigned himself, something new began to happen. When Haratin guards delivered his meals, they were flashing him the victory sign. Unbeknownst to him, IRA was leading thousands-strong protests on his behalf. Haratin were marching in the streets. His arrest had become a source of tension between whites and blacks in offices, markets, and mosques, at military bases where Haratin soldiers clashed with their white officers. Feelings that had gone unsaid for generations spilled out into the open.

The authorities kept up their pressure on Biram, even calling him before a judge to force him to renounce the burning. But the judge concluded that the act wasn't in violation of Mauritanian law. He still wasn't released.

While Biram was in prison, friends of the president visited his cell to encourage him to give conciliatory public statements. He resisted their promises of immediate pardon. The police chief summoned him to his office, treating him as if they were old friends, and said that President Aziz was a good man, and that it would be possible to work things out if only Biram apologized. He refused, and went back to his cell to wait to die or be freed. He couldn't let down his allies on the outside. He couldn't let down his father. His faith, unwavering in its absolute certainty of a God on his side, allowed him to say no again and again, resisting what most people would agree to.

I admired his certainty, and couldn't fathom it. I had first found Biram's name through a night of online research into slavery in West Africa; I was looking for who, if anyone, was trying to stop the practice. I came across a brief clip about the book burning. His daring in the face of an inimical regime was remarkable, and evidence that he was motivated by something deeper. "God was here

during the book burning. This is a permanent fight between the bad and the good," he told me when we met.
Commitment to a struggle often had elements of religious faith underpinning it, and understandably so—how
else could you explain away the suffering required to fight
for what you believed was fair? You had to think it was
merely a trial that God had put on the path to greater reward. There had to be a sense that the scales of justice
were tipping toward your cause, and an equal conviction
that the scales were tipping away from your opponents.
For years, I had been asking where God was in the conflicts and crimes I had reported on in Africa. I wasn't
convinced the scales were tipping at all.

Four months after arresting him, the government gave
up and told Biram he would be released. He could leave
that same day. As Biram walked out of the prison he simply thought, *I win*. A scrawl of black paint now marked a
wall near where the burning took place as "Shar'a Biram,"
or Biram Avenue. But the toll of Biram's bravery on his
family would linger. His wife had not known that Biram
was going to burn the books, though she wasn't surprised
either. When the police came for her husband, Leila had
already sent their children to her mother's home. She had
wanted to accompany Biram to jail, but there were too
many people in their house when he was arrested. Some
were friends, but there were other people present she did
not know. She worried some of them were plainclothes
policemen. She decided to stay and guard their things.
During the burning, she was proud of Biram. In its aftermath, she was terrified.

Their landlord evicted Leila and the children soon after
Biram went to prison. Another one agreed to rent her
a house, but he warned her that neighbors and imams
in the area had tried to dissuade him from allowing her
to move in. After hearing about the neighborhood campaign, Leila decided against going there. She was out of
options. Activists and relatives sent her money to buy cement. She was going to have to construct her own house,
not far from where the burning happened. With the help
of friends, her family began to build. The entire experience was surreal. One moment she had been busy but
happy, taking care of Biram and their little ones and everyone else, too—other activists, her own siblings and
parents—and then everything had been thrown out of
place. She felt alone. Her sisters could not stop crying.
Leila and the children moved into the house when it was
only halfway complete.

Biram returned home an enemy of the state. His face
was now known to anyone who watched television or
read the news. There was nowhere to hide if he had
wanted to. The arrest made his work more difficult.
"There are no funds; we have total need," he said. While
his actions had made Biram a hero to human rights
organizations—Front Line Defenders and the United Nations both honored him that year, and cheering IRA
supporters met him at the airport to welcome him when
he returned from receiving the awards in Dublin and New
York—donations were irregular and never enough. IRA
had to rely on gifts from patrons, mainly sympathetic civil
servants, to finance their activities. Because the Mauri-

tanian government refused to allow IRA to register as a nongovernmental organization, it was impossible to solicit funding through domestic and international grants. Biram refused to let that stop his work.

He was seeking allies among the country's large population of Afro-Mauritanians, black Muslims who faced systemic racism but who had not been enslaved by White Moors. Biram argued that, like Haratin, Afro-Mauritanians had suffered for their dark skin. Yet much separated the two groups. Though Afro-Mauritanians struggled to obtain equal education and employment opportunities and political representation, they tended to look down on Haratin because of their origins in slavery. And they regarded them with suspicion for their connection with White Moors. There was an ugly, difficult history. During the late eighties and early nineties, the government committed ethnic cleansing of some groups of Afro-Mauritanians and used Haratin soldiers to kill and torture them. The government also forcibly expelled about 100,000 Afro-Mauritanians to Senegal and Mali. The collective memory of these events persisted.

Haratin were equally suspicious. They pointed out that Afro-Mauritanians had also once owned slaves, and aligned themselves with White Moor slave owners when it was convenient. After centuries of forced integration, Haratin shared a language and, to an extent, a culture with their captors, and many were reluctant to disavow their link to the privileged class. Their cultural identity had not been predominantly forged by race. As a result, their activists had seen slavery as a problem distinct from racism.

But Biram saw slavery and racism as inextricable, and an alliance between the two groups as politically compelling. Together, they represented more than 70 percent of the population. The government was evidently concerned by the prospect. While Biram was in prison, the police told him that his greatest offense was promoting an alliance between Haratin and Afro-Mauritanians. There was no reason to unite, they said. Haratin were a special group in a special situation. Afro-Mauritanians had nothing to do with them. He disagreed. "It is a link among all victims of slavery, racism, and discrimination," he said. To his delight, the protests outside his prison cell marked the first time that Haratin and Afro-Mauritanians marched together.

When Biram now woke up in the morning, he immediately asked his wife, if she was not still sleeping herself, or a bodyguard, how many people were waiting for him in the salon downstairs. He then washed up, put on a bubu, and walked a few feet from their bedroom into the upstairs salon, where he sat on the carpeted floor with an embroidered pillow behind him. His rambling house, the one Leila built, looked like an unfinished manor, with exposed foundations and missing walls. A thick concrete staircase curved between the two floors. A terrace, essentially a room off the kitchen without an outer wall, extended over the dusty road below. Most of the times I was there a radio on the terrace seemed to playing Celine Dion on loop.

Biram's resolve lent him the appearance of being honest

and incorruptible. When I first met him on a Sunday afternoon in January 2014, he was at the home of an IRA
vice president, wearing a cheap tan suit and settled on
her worn couch, casually holding court among the activists roaming in and out of the house as a fan turned
slowly overhead. A television crackled in the background.
We talked a little about a recent sit-in IRA had held in
front of the justice ministry, and then he, his vice president Brahim, two of Biram's bodyguards, and I squeezed
into a car to go run some errands. Biram had decided to
run for president in the upcoming June election and was
dropping off his campaign literature at the offices of various radio stations and websites, stopping to chat with the
journalists. He was at ease with the reporters, simultane-
ously charming and forthright. I already felt comfortable
with him.

Biram's outward confidence hid an unrelenting anxiety.
"Sometimes I feel doubt," he admitted. The responsibility
of leading IRA could be overwhelming. He was frustrated
with himself for not having groomed a successor yet to
lead the struggle should anything happen to him, someone who could speak to people and move them. And
he was aware of the hurdles he still faced. "When I see
the total power of the authorities, the religious power,
economic power, military power, security power, media
power, all its power, against my organization, and I don't
even have money to buy soap . . . ," he said. He wasn't
exaggerating; he and his wife were always sharing tea,
milk, food, whatever they had, with whoever stopped by,
announced or not. "But it reassures me when I see peo-

ple resist against all the state's actions in spite of their economic situations," he went on. "They don't have anything. Despite that, they resist."

I wanted to understand how, in the twenty-first century, it was possible for a wide swathe of a society to condone slavery. As I tried to find a slave owner who would talk to me, Brahim, the schoolteacher and IRA vice president, put me in touch with Abdel Nasser Ould Ethmane, a political adviser to the African Union and a cofounder of SOS Slaves. Ethmane was in his early fifties, and had tan skin not much lighter than some Haratin and salt-and-pepper hair. He received me warmly. He owned a slave for much of his life; relatives gave him one as a child. Despite his abolitionist work, he had little shame about it, rather a kind of nostalgia, and was exceedingly open. "Slaves ensured the comfort of the master and his family," Ethmane said. "They spared them the manual tasks that White Moor society considers repugnant or demeaning: fetching water, preparing food, herding cattle." They also served more intimate roles, he said, "making the master laugh, massaging him, and ensuring his sexual pleasure, if so desired. Some slaves who assimilated the attitudes and behavior of their masters eventually gained the respect and consideration of the family. The others were insulted, sometimes beaten."

Ethmane's slave was now legally free, but he worked for relatives and still believed that he belonged to Ethmane. "The slaves who still serve my family are no longer constrained by force, only by economic necessity and, I would say, a very strong emotional link," he explained. "Masters and slaves live together, build relationships from generation to generation. Most children of masters were breast-fed and raised by slave nannies; they will later treat them as second mothers. It is a complex link that is very difficult to break."

I didn't doubt the bond between slave owners and the people they enslaved, but I found his romanticizing of the relationship disturbing. It seemed to me that, even though he was now an abolitionist, he was glossing over his memories to assuage his own guilt. White Moors' fear of a changing world was not unfounded. The Mauritanian social order would be upended if slavery were completely abolished, and White Moors would have to perform their own menial tasks and pay for labor on an unprecedented scale. Their concepts of race and hierarchy would be shattered. "The former master needs therapy more than the former slave, because of trauma resulting from the rupture between his sense of racial superiority and the necessity of the modern world," Ethmane went on. So, in public, he said, White Moors echoed the government's line: "Slavery no longer exists, and talk of it suggests manipulation by the West, an act of enmity toward Islam, or influence from the worldwide Jewish conspiracy." Ethmane's sense of fragility as a White Moor was honest, but seemed to me stunningly ignorant of the emotional and physical damage Haratin carried.

If this was a progressive White Moor, was there hope for the ones who were not as evolved?

• • •

Many Mauritanians existed somewhere on a continuum between slavery and freedom. There was outright subjugation; there was indentured servitude, like the sharecropping that prevailed in Biram's village; and there was the ex-slaves' struggle with what was politely referred to as the "vestiges of slavery." The situation for former slaves on the fringes of Nouakchott or in rural areas was dire. They faced discrimination when looking for work, and, without education and living in poverty, they risked becoming enslaved again. Because much of the economy was informal, even those who did find work were often exploited and poorly paid.

In Nouakchott, among friends, people admitted to owning slaves, but with strangers they claimed that the slaves were relatives. Yet the evidence of it was there. In a grocery store, I came across a White Moor family with a Haratin girl who fetched their purchases and then followed them to the car, where she sat in the backseat cradling the family's child. I left the store and returned to Brahim's car. He turned eagerly to me and said, "Did you see? Did you see their slave?" In front of the opulent house of a prominent White Moor journalist, he pointed out a shack that was empty except for a mat. "It's the type of place where slaves sleep," Brahim told me.

There had been a few Haratin politicians, but the government remained dominated by White Moors. In 2013, Messaoud Ould Boulkheir, a self-possessed Haratin who was the president of the National Assembly, announced that "slavery is alive and well in Mauritania." The government did not respond.

One morning in February 2014, I went to see Biram's former boss Boubacar Messaoud, the leader of SOS Slaves, to talk about his work. His office was in a cool whitewashed building on a quiet street. He founded the organization in 1995 and had been its leader ever since. In his late sixties with a snowy beard and dark creased skin, Messaoud was a former slave who went on to study engineering and architecture in Bamako, the capital of Mali, and in Moscow. He had the didactic air of a professor and could talk endlessly about slavery.

SOS aided slaves who escaped their masters and petitioned the government and the imams to address the problem, but the group stopped short of aggressively confronting the authorities. He had worked closely with Biram, whom he considered passionate and expressive, when the younger activist joined SOS. "It's a generational difference," Messaoud said. Biram was leading a movement of young people driven by a sense of urgency; what they were doing now would have been impossible ten years earlier. "We did not have the same conception about the fight against slavery," Messaoud said. Their approaches did sometimes converge. He, Biram, and an IRA vice president once held a hunger strike over two days in a Nouakchott police station, in the police chief's office, until the police put three different slave owners in jail. (The police chief would only meet with them outside the station now.) He said he had resisted several attempts from the government to pit his organization against IRA. He didn't agree with Biram burning the books, but he supported the sentiment.

Biram told me that he also didn't advocate violence, but he thought it was inevitable as long as the government kept cracking down on activists. He gave the example of Nelson Mandela's militant beginnings with Umkhonto we Sizwe. "Haratin have to take power. White Moors have no choice. They have to change," he said. "But the price will be heavy. Both sides will pay a tough price. White Moors have not accepted that Haratin will not put up with their illicit privilege forever. Haratin will one day say, 'Stop,' and there will be a confrontation. The price Haratin will have to pay is blood."

In our meeting, I asked Messaoud if he knew how many people were currently enslaved in Mauritania. He responded that the government played a game with visitors when they asked them the same question. They told visitors to ask activists how many slaves there were, and how many they had freed. "We don't know," Messaoud said. "The state should know. Our business is just to help people when they come to us."

Nevertheless, some thought that Mauritanian society was slowly evolving. In 2013, IRA organized a "caravan of freedom" of buses and cars to the far east and crossed the country back to the capital over twelve days, stopping in towns and villages to have public discussions on slavery. "Everywhere people came to us," Brahim told me. They learned of slavery cases in three towns, and held sit-ins in front of the police stations until officers detained the slave owners.

People used to brag about having many slaves and camels, Mohamed Said Ould Hemody, a former Mauritanian ambassador to the United States, told me. His late father, an Afro-Mauritanian, owned slaves. It was now taboo to say such a thing. "This is a very important phase," he said. "People are saying this is the start of something." As the first director of the country's National Human Rights Commission from 2007 to 2010, he had seen many cases of "open slavery." During that time, he hired Biram to work for him and they freed several slaves together, like two crusading superheroes rescuing the vulnerable. They worked together for just over a year until Hemody was pressured by the government to let Biram go. Hemody resigned soon afterward.

Several former slaves that Biram had freed lived in his house, including the two boys he rescued from the slave owner who was released after two months. I found one of them, Moctar Ould Sidi, playing soccer one sunset in a field near the house. Shy and polite, he had a head of bushy curls, hazel eyes, and glowing, reddish skin, and he was wearing athletic clothes and shoes. He was fifteen. "My mother was a slave, and I was a slave," he said. In the house of a wealthy family in Nouakchott, Sidi cleaned, washed the dishes, ran errands. He had no name in that house. He was called *abd*, or slave. He slept by himself in a tent outside. "I didn't have any right to study, any right to sleep when I want, any right to play when I want," he said. I asked him if the family members ever hit him. "Always, always, always," he said. Sidi recalled that his masters were generous with their children. "They gave them money, they gave them good clothes, and they sent them to school," he said. "They never gave me that." Instead, they berated and beat his mother in his presence. Still, she told him to stay, believing it was his best option.

When he was twelve, a friend of his mother took him to an IRA representative, who led him to Biram. He and Biram went to the police station together. "My mother was angry at me when I left my masters," Sidi recalled. "To her, she is a slave, I am a slave, and we have to be slaves—she did not understand." Their relationship was slowly improving. His mother told him his three siblings were not enslaved and that they lived with her, but Sidi sounded uncertain. "Now I feel that I am a person because before that I was not a person. I was nothing," he said. "And now I feel like I'm like all boys in this country. I feel like I'm free."

The Mauritanian government was taking symbolic measures to appease critics. It had acknowledged the lingering effects of slavery. In 2014, it opened the National Solidarity Agency for the Fight Against the Vestiges of Slavery, for Integration, and for the Fight Against Poverty. One day Brahim took me to the office of Hamdi Ould Mahjoub, a slight White Moor with glasses who ran the agency. I expected to be made to wait for hours, especially since I had an abolitionist with me. Instead, the Haratin assistant, an older man, went into Mahjoub's suite to tell him we were there, and then immediately ushered us into the plush room. He and Brahim greeted each other like, if not old friends, at least like people who had known each other a long time.

As Mahjoub and I shook hands, he looked me in the

eye and, after asking me where I was from, said that former slaves were no worse off than black Americans. "I will give you an example," he said. "Today in the United States, forty percent of prisoners are black Americans. And the percentage of black Americans who are unemployed is not proportional to the percentage of black Americans in society. Those are the kinds of problems we have generation to generation." I didn't react, but inside I was rolling my eyes. His attempt to deflect from his country's troubles by focusing on the ones in mine was a favorite tactic of despots and politicians alike. He said that the agency was working on a program to build clinics and improve access to water. "After the Civil War in the United States, the government promised to buy each slave family a mule and forty acres, but it did not," he said. He began laughing. "There are donkeys everywhere we can use."

I asked Mahjoub how his organization planned to help current slaves. "If the agency has evidence of a case of slavery, any practice of slavery, we have the authority to be the advocate for the slave. But since the agency was created, no cases have been reported to us," he said. There was a silence. I turned off my tape recorder, and then turned it on. But did slavery exist? I asked him again. He stopped, too. "Slavery as an institution," he began again, "as something accepted by society, does not exist."

Biram felt he needed to show foreign governments the hypocrisy of what was happening inside Mauritania. But to convince his countrymen of his cause, "I always knew that my fight had to be inside religion, not outside it," he said. Framing the country's slavery crisis in terms of human rights was not enough. "I wanted to bring principles from the Koran to convince people that there are two Islams: the real Islam and the wrong interpretation of Islam." He believed it was easy to find ideals like equality, tolerance, and freedom of expression in his religion.

It was early 2014, and he was sitting cross-legged in the upstairs salon of his house as he talked. Activists and other men, mostly middle-aged and older in varying states of health, filtered into the room throughout the day, as many as twenty filling the small space. Some had come to ask for money, others for medicine, and yet others for advice. Other visitors to his home were just lonely and wanted the company of a lively group, and yet others simply had nothing to do: no work, no school. (One day not long ago, eight people came to ask for money; the night before, he did not have money to buy sugar for his tea.) Biram was in his element in front of an audience, even while suffering from a toothache, and Leila brought him a breakfast of bread and tea. As he recounted accosting a policeman during one story, the men assembled laughed and murmured their approval.

"People come to talk to me about all kinds of crimes: rape, children taken from them, land taken away, racism, all in relation to slavery," Biram said. "They come because we are the only people who listen to them. We are the only organization that challenges the power and the dominant group publicly, and we make the most sacrifices." Activists would go with the petitioners to the local government, to the courts, to the police stations, to help them get justice. Sometimes people would come from afar, from within the interior of the country, for help. IRA would gather money and send an activist or two back with them to their home towns to help resolve the problem.

When I asked Biram if he ever felt resentment toward the many people who needed him, he didn't say anything for a long moment. "I feel frustrated because I don't have enough time for my family, for my children, for myself," he said. He could feel his wife's and children's disappointment. He rarely listened to music like he once did, and barely had the time to regularly read the Koran. "God has a central place in my thoughts and in my hopes, and God is a central foundation of my principles, in how I think about sacrifice and about my humanity," he said. When he was in Mauritania, his work consumed him. Even going to the market in Nouakchott resulted in him being recognized and mobbed. When he was in Europe or the United States, he could walk freely, think, and write.

A few activists complained to me about his frequent travels, but Biram said he longed for privacy and the freedom to do what he wanted unnoticed. He sometimes regretted the fame he had acquired in Mauritania, and idealized the anonymity he once had. "Now everybody is looking at me, looking at my wife. My name is more famous than IRA," he said. "I feel like I have sacrificed my life, the lives of my family, my friends, to give life to others. The fight against slavery is a fight to the death." His words poured out in a rush. "After one month here, I'm exhausted because I listen to painful stories every day from people about their problems, stories that make me physically and mentally weak," he said. "I cannot do sports, or even walk for leisure. There is no rest."

I asked Biram what his dreams were for the future of Haratin. "I don't have a dream," he said defiantly. "I have ambitions, objectives I want to accomplish. I'm awake, not sleeping." He believed that Haratin would take control of their destiny. It was impossible for his people to continue tolerating oppression. "They don't give us opportunities, they don't help us, they keep crushing our pacifist actions," he said, ticking off the crimes of White Moors. Haratin were fed up. What else could they do but revolt?

On a January afternoon in Nouakchott in 2014, some 300 people filled an open-air pavilion that reached up two stories with balconies on the second level. Men in crinkled linen bubus sat on one side of the room, smoking and talking; women in yellow, blue, and purple hijabs sat on the opposite side of the room, which was decorated in shades of white and blue. Loud Mauritanian rap and hypnotic traditional music played on speakers in front of a stage. The mood of the crowd was expectant and a little restless. Friends greeted each other, and IRA activists led prominent guests, former senators and government ministers, to the front row. Suddenly applause commenced. Biram, surrounded by an entourage of security, emerged in a fitted black suit with faint pinstripes. The audience stood up and watched him acknowledge the front-row dignitaries and then take a seat at a table on the stage. Leila sat beside him. Activists fussed around the table, body-guards tripped over themselves as they took posts on the stage, and journalists stuck multiplying recorders and cameras in front of him. Biram looked nonplussed, a smile on his face as he surveyed the crowd. He placed a hand on his heart when he caught the eyes of various supporters. It seemed that he had been waiting for this day all his life. Biram was announcing that he was running for president of Mauritania. The elections were five months away.

"Today we are going to make history," an activist on the stage announced to applause. A band played a cheerful set, and then, still seated, Biram began to speak. He expressed gratitude for those who had been with him when the government demonized him after the book burning and put him in prison. His intellectual project to end slavery and help Haratin achieve their human rights had led him to this point, he told the crowd. No longer would Islam be associated with slavery and racism. "We put Mauritania in front of the international forum. We put Mauritania on the path to excellence. We put Mauritania on the path to goodness," he declared. "We put Mauritania on the path to being a respected country. This human rights project has led to a spiritual project to purify our religion, to discuss our religion, and to consider our religion as a way to freedom, not slavery. We are working to bring people back to the original Islam: the Islam of freedom, the Islam of tolerance, the Islam of peace." The audience clapped and whistled.

"I am determined to win this race in front of my friends, my admirers, and even my adversaries. We will win," he went on. The excitement in the room reached a fevered pitch. "I decided to trade the happiness of my family and my friends for a Mauritania without slavery, racism, and corruption." He promised to lead with honesty. "Biram will stay Biram! Biram will stay Biram!" he roared. He didn't mention the difficulties that lay ahead with the election, such as the fact that a majority of blacks lacked the identity cards required to vote.

He had channeled his belief in revolution into a quixotic run for president. He used to think that the opposition politicians were doing all they could for marginalized people in Mauritania. After the burning, he realized that they and the ruling party were two sides of the same coin. I couldn't tell if he actually believed he would win—he probably wasn't sure himself. He wouldn't admit any doubts aloud. But his arrogance was seductive. He was the first ever authentic Haratin candidate for president, one who said he was truly independent from White Moors' ideology and lies. The others had basically been White Moors with black skin. He was going to force the government to admit that slavery still existed.

When the ceremony ended, bodyguards huddled around Biram as the crowd surged toward him, taking cell phone photos and screaming his name. Biram paused briefly for photographs before ducking into a car outside. Afterward, the hall, still full of people, felt empty.

In June, Biram lost the election. His detractors, and even some allies, claimed that he was interested primarily in self-promotion. Biram saw the election as a forum to dis-

cuss slavery and racism. But most of the opposition, concerned about the possibility of government fraud, pulled
out, and, in any case, many black Mauritanians never received their identity cards. Biram's ambition, as admirable
as it was, made him unreasonably hardheaded, keeping
him in a race that he should have exited. He came in
second to Aziz, with 9 percent of the vote. He filed an
appeal with the Constitutional Council, arguing that in a
fair election he would have received at least 35 percent.

Still, the work continued. In November 2014, Biram,
Brahim, and several other activists conducted a caravan
tour through the Senegal River Valley, stopping in communities to talk with Haratin and Afro-Mauritanian farmers about their land rights. The government had been
selling off land that blacks had long occupied to cronies,
local elites, and foreign investors. The activists wanted
to ensure black farmers didn't lose the source of their
livelihoods, and their ancestral homes; they were vulnerable to being enslaved or entering serf-like relationships
if they had nowhere else to go and needed work as
the new landowners moved in. Government develop-
ment assistance in the valley was essentially nonexistent.
Afro-Mauritanians were as vulnerable as Haratin. Most
of them were, or were related to, refugees who returned
after the ethnic cleansing and deportations of the 1980s
and 1990s; without identity documents, their freedom of
movement and even claim to citizenship were limited. Biram again saw the link uniting these two groups in struggle. The political climate was tense. Mohamed Cheikh
Ould Mkhaitir, a young White Moor blogger, had just

been imprisoned for apostasy after he wrote an article challenging the way Mauritanian elite interpreted Islam to uphold the country's caste system, dividing even White Moors from birth.

When the caravan reached the outskirts of the city of Rosso, a contingent of local police confronted and then arrested them. Biram, Brahim, and the rest were charged with protesting without official authorization, belonging to an unrecognized organization, and stirring public unrest. President Aziz was said to have approved of the arrests. Biram had begun to think that he had become invincible on some level, and had immunity from arbitrary imprisonment and torture by a government that knew better than to persecute a man who had become a leader of black Mauritanians. But with his fight against unequal land distribution, what he called "land slavery," he had gone too far. I was in New York when I learned of their arrests, after wondering why Brahim wasn't responding to any of my e-mails. He, Biram, and another man named Djiby Sow had been sentenced to two years in prison, and then moved to a jail in the remote, hot town of Aleg to serve their sentences.

Their families and other activists were allowed infrequent visits. At one point, Biram was evacuated to the hospital for chest pains. By November 2015, he had been moved to a prison in Nouakchott to be closer to his doctor. His family and friends were visiting often and bringing him home-cooked meals. Haby, who owed her freedom to Biram, felt relief that he was now close to home. She was doing well. Her husband was home on military leave and she happily devoted herself to him, and her son was thriving. It felt wrong to her that the man who had helped her save herself was now fighting for his own liberty. Their positions had bitterly reversed. The government continued to claim that IRA was spreading "racist propaganda." Yet, without irony, the government passed a new law in August 2015 declaring slavery a "crime against humanity" and doubling maximum prison terms for slave owners to twenty years. When a court upheld Biram's sentence that same month, he released an open letter. "Today I am writing to you from the prison cell I am kept in for speaking out to end this cruel trade," he wrote. "I refuse to give up. I refuse to be silenced. I refuse to abandon my country, and those whose lives have been ruined by slavery."

Nine months later, Biram and Brahim were released from prison after the supreme court there overturned their sentences. I was surprised and grateful. So were Biram's supporters: Haby and other members of IRA who hadn't lost hope in the eventual return of their leader, but whose faith had nearly been broken by the long days he was kept from them. The following month, he and Brahim visited the United States. The Department of State had invited them to Washington, D.C., to recognize their efforts. Then–secretary of state John Kerry gave them one of that year's Trafficking in Persons Report Heroes awards, which were given to people fighting human trafficking. I went to see them in D.C. and New York. Biram looked tired when I first saw him; it was the height of Ramadan and he was hungry and weak, waiting for sundown to eat. After his stay in prison, he was feeling disillusioned about his country, but he told me that he was planning to run for president again in 2019. He had no doubt, naturally, that he would win. There was much to do when they returned to Mauritania: try to register IRA again, carry out another caravan, keep freeing slaves.

3

NIGERIA

Nobody Rescued Them

"DOES ANYONE want to follow me?" Rebecca asked the girls around her. She looked down and saw Boko Haram gunmen on foot keeping pace with the trucks. Her friend Saraye told her to be quiet, that she was being crazy. What about the appendix operation Rebecca was still healing from? Rebecca was getting angry. Why didn't they want to go with her? How could they just stay behind for whatever fate awaited them? "If I die, at least my parents will be able to see my body," she said. Saraye said she was afraid. Rebecca faltered for a moment. She felt like she could burst into a million pieces right then, collapse on the floor in tears and never get back up. Instead, she looked at her friend and told her she would pray for her, and asked Saraye to pray for her, too. Saraye said she would.

A few minutes later, when the truck was passing another giant tree, Rebecca jumped. She fell in a tangle of branches and bushes, and then started running. Men were behind and in front of her. Several of them started shooting. She crept behind a tree and lay down on her stomach, waiting until some of them passed. She started running again. When she saw more men coming, she hid behind another tree. When they all passed, she ran through the night until daybreak. In the dark forest, the trees looked like specters, hovering, tentacled ghosts, and the bushes like waiting monsters. The ground was hard and painful. At dawn, Rebecca saw smoke curling through the trees. She felt almost sick with hope. She followed the smoke until she reached a village. The people there asked her if she was one of the students from Chibok; they had already heard about the kidnapping.

The villagers took Rebecca home on a motorcycle. When she arrived at her house, an hour's drive from where she had found the village, her father emerged, crying. He and Rebecca cried together, holding each other. Her hands and legs were bloody from her fall in the forest. He asked about her nieces. Two of her brother's daughters had also been taken. Altogether, eight girls from her family were missing. She told him that she hadn't seen them, that she didn't think they had escaped. Parents of classmates stopped in throughout the day, asking her about their daughters. Each time, she told them she hadn't seen their children, her friends. The parents cried in response. Rebecca could barely speak to them.

Her school was little more than dust. Boko Haram had burned nearly everything, but they had left something behind for the town. When the men were gathering the girls to take them away, they had demanded each girl give them her spare shoes. As they left, the men lined up the sandals in front of the rubble. When the administrators and parents saw the shoes, they stared at them in disbelief. The girls had truly vanished, as if the Holy Spirit had come and taken them himself.

Elder heard about the kidnapping the next morning. Residents of the area called him with the news. There were hunters in and around Chibok, local vigilantes loosely affiliated with the CJTF, but they couldn't have expected the hundreds of heavily armed insurgents who overtook the school that night. Elder was trying to stay calm, but he couldn't make the anxiety go away. Why wasn't the military protecting his people? He was tired of asking the question.

A day after the abduction, the Nigerian military said it had rescued nearly all the girls. But a day later, not only did the military retract its claim—it had not, in fact, rescued any of the girls—but also the number of girls it said was missing, just over 100, turned out to be triple that. Over 300 girls were stolen that night. The kidnapped girls were both Christian and Muslim; their only offense was attending school.

In the wake of the military's utter failure, parents banded together and raised money to rent motorbikes and send the fathers into the forest to search for the girls. The group came across villagers who persuaded the parents to turn back. They told the fathers they had seen the girls nearby, but the insurgents were too well armed. Many of the parents had just bows and arrows.

Two weeks later, the military still had not found any schoolgirls. Elder decided to lead a group of vigilantes to try and locate them. They had received tips about the girls' whereabouts and ventured to villages around Sambisa Forest. He and about a hundred vigilantes moved together in nine trucks. Elder and his boys went to an area called Alagarno, where the girls had been sighted. They found nothing there. It was too dangerous for them to go farther into the forest without backup. They had their locally made guns and they didn't know how many militants they would encounter, or what weapons they would be carrying. They called off the rescue attempt. Chibok didn't fall under their jurisdiction. They had just wanted to help. "It really pained me like it was my own daughter. Because these poor girls, they were there to get knowledge," Elder said. "It disturbed me. I would love to see these kids back with their families, although the damage has been done. The damage has been done. Even if they are not alive, let the parents see the corpses."

Deborah Ishaya was one of the schoolgirls taken that night. It was noon when her group reached the terrorists' camp on the day following the abduction. The militants forced her classmates to cook food, but she couldn't eat. Two hours later, she pulled two friends close and told them they should run. One of them hesitated and said they should try to escape at night. Deborah insisted, and they fled behind some trees. The guards spotted them and called out for them to return, but the girls kept running. No one followed them. They reached a village late

187

at night and slept at a friendly stranger's house. When they woke, they called their families.

Deborah could not tell me any more than that. I had located her father's phone number several days after the abduction. I was working in Senegal and was desperate to find people to talk to about the kidnapping, which was being undercovered in the press. After I called several contacts in northeastern Nigeria, I finally found Deborah. Only eighteen, she was deeply traumatized. Her cousins and her friends were still missing, and she was trying to understand how she was alive and back home. What she knew she could do, she said, was pray and fast. Then pray and fast again.

"I want to go back to school but I am afraid," Sarah Lawan, another girl who escaped, told me. "Up until now I can see those people with guns standing above me, forcing me to enter their vehicles. I don't want to be at gunpoint again." Sarah wanted to be a doctor. She had a strong and energetic voice, even on a fragile phone line from Chibok. Her mother, Taditha, never had the chance to go to school because her parents could not afford to send her. Taditha wanted Sarah to "be somebody who could give a helping hand to the family after completing her education," she said. Sarah was nineteen. She had jumped out of a truck with a friend. "I thought I'd rather die by jumping out of the truck than from a gun," she said. Her father had died five years earlier, and she didn't want her mother to have to grieve her, too. "I'm still thinking of all the girls who have not yet returned," her mother told me.

In the meantime, as in so many other ways in Nigeria, each community had to fend for itself. For a while after the abduction, more than fifty girls trickled back into town, after they leapt off trucks or ran away while fetching water. That trickle soon stopped. "Nobody rescued them," a Chibok government official said of the girls who made it back. "I want you to stress this point. Nobody rescued them. They escaped on their own accord. This is painful, you know?" Officials still did not have an exact number of how many were missing because girls from nearby villages had also gone to the school to take exams. Once the militants burned down the school, all records of the students were lost.

Three weeks after the kidnapping, Boko Haram released a video claiming responsibility for the kidnapping. "I have your girls. By Allah, I will sell them in the market," its leader, Abubakar Shekau, said. Parents were hearing rumors that members of the group were using their daughters as sex slaves. As time stretched on with no news of the remaining girls, violence committed by Boko Haram and the security forces continued to plague Chibok. At least eighteen parents of the missing girls would die, many from violence or stress-related health reasons. And some of them, their neighbors said, simply passed away from grief and broken hearts.

I traveled to Chibok myself a month after the abduction. When the girls were taken, I was reporting and learning French in Dakar, Senegal. I wanted to get to Chibok. I had visited Maiduguri the previous June to report on the insurgency and the Nigerian government's resulting counteroffensive, a security operation that placed three northeastern states, including Borno State, the capital of which was Maiduguri, under a state of emergency as troops launched attacks on Boko Haram camps. The military had cut phone and Internet lines, and while residents were glad for the intervention, it was like living in the dark. Unable to communicate with the outside world and even among themselves without physically finding each other, residents of the northeast found it impossible to know what was happening beyond their doorsteps. Gunshots, a bomb blast: Was it Boko Haram or a military attack? Were the hundreds of men the military disappeared actually terrorists? Even the young boys? What was happening in Giwa Barracks, the military base in Maiduguri where men who were once kept told stories of torture and killings? And was the government, as it claimed, really winning the war?

The military had since restored phone lines in Borno State. But other things had become difficult. The sole commercial airline that flew to Maiduguri cancelled the route at the end of 2013 after Boko Haram attacked the airport. Driving eight hours from Kano, the largest city in the north, was the best alternative. I would have to take the bus, a Nigerian friend and journalist warned me. Taking a private taxi would make me look like a lucrative target. Once I reached Maiduguri, though, my journey would have to stop. The road to Chibok was so hazardous that Borno State's governor visited the town only with a heavy military escort. Much of the northeast was now isolated. It all raised a chilling question: What was happening there that we could not see?

I went to Chibok with a friend and resident of the town, who hosted me in his home. The road out of Maiduguri was desolate: Even on a market day, only a few cars, trucks, and minivan taxis were found on the eighty-mile route, hurtling past buildings that were now burned shells. Torched vehicles idled in the middle of the road, all traces of their passengers gone. Cars honked at each other to encourage passage in a kind of informal safety system. Boys rode on bikes with bows and arrows tucked under their arms. A series of checkpoints stopped commuters; some were manned by the military, others by the CJTF. The vigilantes were more disorganized but savvier. They casually waved machetes at drivers and demanded they turn on their windshield wipers. Militants had been hiding weapons under car hoods, preventing the wipers from working.

My guide was a man named Ayuba Yamta, who I had first interviewed over the phone about the kidnapping—some of his friends' daughters had been taken—and then began talking to regularly about his town. We visited a few girls who had escaped in the early days of the abduction in a village outside of Chibok called Jajel. Ten girls who lived in Jajel were kidnapped; all but one managed to return home. Comfort Ayuba, who was eighteen, told me that Boko Haram members had realized there was not enough space in their trucks to take all the girls, and forced a Christian girl to lie flat on the ground. They pointed a gun at her and asked if she would change her faith. She responded she would not, even if they killed her. The men told her to run away and not look back.

Rejoice Yaga, a fourteen-year-old with a dusting of acne, recalled that when the girls reached the Boko Haram camp, the group's weapons and vehicles, along with a refrigerator, were kept in plain sight.

My friend Ayuba then drove me to his house, and we had dinner with his wife and children on the front lawn. As night fell, the landscape turned to utter blackness. Chibok hadn't had electricity in a very long time; Boko Haram had destroyed a nearby electrical grid, and government neglect had left it unrepaired. Ayuba's family wasn't using a generator. I couldn't see anything in front of me. My host and his wife, however, continued eating and talking with friends who had dropped by, as if they had acquired a deeper sense of sight after so many days of darkness. They gave me their bedroom that night. I couldn't sleep much and was relieved when the sun rose. He took me back to Maiduguri a few hours later.

That same week, Elder picked me up at my hotel on the way to his headquarters. A new pack of volunteers was squeezed into the back of the truck, their legs pressed together as they sat in two rows facing each other. They wore T-shirts and sunglasses, with handkerchiefs and guns slung around their necks. They were joking and laughing, and they watched with amusement as I climbed into the vehicle.

"I was sitting in my office preparing paperwork for my boys who went for training when I received a call from one of my chairmen," Elder said as he drove. His colleague told Elder that he seen some of the Boko Haram members they had been looking for at a bank in town. Elder and his boys immediately rushed over, but the suspects had already left. So he dropped off several of his boys at the parking lot, where they set up a checkpoint in the hopes of catching them if they returned.

Elder put on the truck's siren and swerved between the narrow lanes. As we sped through CJTF checkpoints, the young men at the barriers saluted him. Elder suspected the Boko Haram suspects would next go to the market to buy food. He had put members of the other sectors on alert so they would be on lookout. The militants slept in the bush, came into town to get money and food, and then went back to their camps. But as soon as Elder's people saw them, they would grab them.

He was worked up about the military that day. "If I were a soldier, I would not go into Sambisa Forest because I wouldn't have enough equipment to fight the insurgents! I withdrew my men from Sambisa because I knew the authorities didn't want to finish this job," he said. The vigilantes couldn't do it alone. They didn't even have proper protective gear or properly functioning weapons. "Sometimes your gun won't even work," Elder went on. It was a miracle only fifteen of his men had been killed so far. The siren blared louder.

We picked up medicine for Elder's youngest daughter, who was very ill with the measles. He was worried about her. His phone rang. The caller was reporting another attack on a village and demanding to know why Elder and his men weren't there. When he hung up, he sighed and his body slackened. "You know, I'm tired of this thing," he said. "We gave the security forces everything—information about the camps, where they are—and they're not doing anything." I asked him if he had given up on finding the girls. "We can't go up to Chibok again," he said.

The year 2014 was among the most lethal since the Boko Haram insurgency began, from the slaughter of dozens of schoolboys in Yobe State, to three bomb blasts in the capital Abuja, to the near daily slaughters in remote villages. Boko Haram continued to lure foot soldiers, despite becoming unpopular among the general north-eastern population. The group offered money and the promise of women, and a vague and messianic vision of a higher purpose.

But the Nigerian government made a mockery of the kidnapped girls and their parents' grief. Then-president Goodluck Jonathan, a Christian Southerner, had always behaved as if the insurgency was a creation of northern Muslim leaders, and thus their problem to solve. It took him more than three weeks to speak publicly about the Chibok abduction, as Nigerians, including mothers of the kidnapped girls, protested in Chibok, Maiduguri, Abuja, and Lagos. Disturbingly, he admitted he did not know where Boko Haram was holding the students, and he blamed the parents for not giving a "clear identity" of their missing daughters. Residents of the northeast had complained frequently of the army's indifference. But their grievances coalesced around the response to the kid-napping. Many of us in Nigeria were devastated. An ac-quaintance called me one morning to tell me his brother had just been killed in a Boko Haram attack. I didn't know how to comfort him. After I hung up, I broke down in my hotel room in Abuja, unable to stop crying. The military claimed that it had broken up a Boko Haram cell that participated in the abduction, and that it was on the verge of rescuing the girls, but the girls who came back saved themselves.

When Boko Haram laid siege to northeastern towns, residents observed that soldiers often abandoned the battles and joined civilians fleeing to safety. Babangida Usman, a senior investigator with Nigeria's National Human Rights Commission, told me most of the soldiers who had been stationed in Chibok were pulled out mere days before. Residents had heard that Boko Haram was coming to the town up to two hours prior to the kidnapping. They had alerted the military, but it only sent more troops hours after the abduction. "People are feeling that the soldiers are playing along with the insurgents," Usman said. There had been reports of military collusion with the terrorists, and President Jonathan once said that Boko Haram had infiltrated both the military and the government.

Almost a year before the abduction, I spent a day in Usman's office in Maiduguri. We spent hours there, in a shabby, bare room talking about the corpses he was counting daily at the city's morgues; the military was dumping the bodies and claiming they were terrorists killed in battle. But the corpses told a different story: They showed signs of torture, like cigarette burns. A window behind his desk let in syrupy afternoon light as we looked through a thick binder filled with the photos of boys and men the military had taken during neighborhood raids. They had ended up at Giwa Barracks, where former detainees said prisoners were starved, shot, beaten, and suffocated to death. Usman, thin and intelligent, was trembling with anger and paranoia. The disappearances and killings had been going on for a long time, and he was worried about the safety of his sources, and his own. By the time of the Chibok abduction in April 2014, 1,500 people had already been killed by the security forces or Boko Haram that year.

For four months after her escape, Rebecca barely left the house. She was having nightmares, frightening, vivid dreams of being taken by Boko Haram again. She wondered about what had happened to her friends and her classmates, what they could be doing, how they were being treated. Had she done enough to try to convince the girls in her truck to jump with her? The thought haunted her. Gradually, her parents brought up the idea of school again. She was close to graduating; she had only two years left. They suggested that she could go to the capital, Abuja, a staid, expansive city of government buildings and planned housing estates, and stay with a cousin she grew up with while she finished there. Rebecca balked. She wasn't ready. She had just started going back to church, where her neighbors told her they were praying for her recovery.

The cousin in Abuja, a man named Emmanuel, was so close to her family she called him her brother. He told her that he was also praying for her, but that it was time to come down and rejoin life. "If I go back to school, it will happen again," Rebecca told him. "It's Abuja," he said. "It won't happen here." After an attack in a town near Chibok, Emmanuel called again and told her to come to the capital immediately. *They may still come carry this girl and go,* he thought, *so it's better she come here.* Most of Rebecca's siblings were married and living in other cities.

When Rebecca started school in September, her first months back tortured her. If someone shouted in class, she stood up in fear. She would inexplicably cry during lessons. When her teachers spoke, she found it hard to pay attention. After a while, when being in class began to seem safer, she could listen better. Some of her classes, like English, math, civics, literature, and economics, were even interesting, taking her mind off the fear that wouldn't release her. She made friends with bright, kind girls with names like Sarah and Rose, and it became a little easier to wake up each day and begin her half-hour walk to school.

Of the almost sixty girls who escaped from Boko Haram after the abduction, she kept in touch with just one. Hauwa attended school a few hours away in the city of Jos, in Nigeria's central plateau. They called each other and talked about their classes, their families, how they were doing. They didn't talk about that night. Rebecca had heard varying stories about what happened to the girls. Some said they were still alive. Others said they had been killed. She heard a girl was buried up to her neck in the dirt and stoned. That one was hard to think about. Another person told her that her classmates had been separated into groups and taken to different places in Cameroon and Chad. "Sometimes you will see her just sit down like this," Emmanuel said, miming someone staring blankly at nothing. "She's thinking about what happened."

There were things Elder couldn't forget. A close colleague of his, who worked alongside him in the CJTF, was ambushed by Boko Haram on the outskirts of the city, along with seven other vigilantes, in 2013. Four of them escaped. The other four, including his friend, died. He was only thirty-five and had a wife and children. A month before the Chibok abduction, Boko Haram raided Giwa Barracks, killing soldiers and freeing the detainees there. Elder lost seven of his boys when they went in to fight the insurgents. The military wouldn't let him carry their bodies out of the base. He was never able to retrieve the corpses for their wives and children, something that haunted him. It was later revealed that the military went on a killing spree after the Boko Haram raid, executing around 600 of the unarmed prisoners at the base, nearly all of whom had not had trials or undergone due process. Most of the people who were held there, including boys as young as eight and elderly men, were innocent of the crimes of which they were accused.

In late 2014, Elder was in low spirits. His daughter with the measles had died, and he had taken a break from his CJTF duties. He didn't know when he would rejoin his colleagues; he was exhausted. The government had claimed to have struck a cease-fire with Boko Haram that would lead to the release of the remaining Chibok schoolgirls. But in October, the militants abducted sixty women and girls from Adamawa State, and then at least thirty boys and girls from Borno State. Boko Haram was now declaring itself the head of a caliphate. There was no truce that Boko Haram recognized. Elder was no longer doing much fieldwork. He was going to run for Senate, he had decided.

But after several arduous months in which Boko Haram captured town after town in the northeast, Elder helped lead the CJTF's operation with the military to recapture the town of Damboa. Things were looking up. I asked him what he thought about the government's proposal to give amnesty to Boko Haram fighters who turned themselves in. He didn't reflect for a moment. "I don't give it, I don't allow it. I don't support any government to give them amnesty," he said. "The government said we are going to rehabilitate them but I know one thing—Boko Haram will never repent."

The militants attempted to invade Maiduguri in January 2015, along with two smaller towns. The assault sent overwhelmed soldiers running away from one of those small towns, which fell to Boko Haram. But Maiduguri held its ground because of the vigilantes who were fighting alongside the military. The night before the siege, Elder had been alerted to Boko Haram activity near the city. By seven the next morning, the militants were trying to enter Maiduguri, and he and other vigilantes were blocking their way. At least eight people died during the attacks, and residents of housing estates located near the clashes had to flee, but the vigilantes were triumphant. Even as much of his state succumbed to the group, Elder was confident again that they would defeat the terrorists.

• • •

In October 2015, I returned to Maiduguri. Elder had lost his Senate race, but he didn't take it personally. He would just try again. He wanted to introduce me to a twenty-six-year-old woman named Fatima Muhammed, the first female member of his unit. After Elder called Fatima repeatedly, she agreed to take a quick break from the canteen she ran in the city and come to the house he owned across the street from the compound his first two wives and all their children shared. Fatima was still fielding calls from demanding customers. Dressed in a maroon hijab that framed her pleasant, rounded face, she would put her phone down, only to have to pick it up again a few minutes later. I asked her why she had joined the CJTF. "They will kill you. They will kill everyone you know," Fatima said of Boko Haram. "That's what motivated me to join."

The group had killed her close friend three years earlier, a man who was like a father to her. And so, even before the CJTF started up in 2013, she had been working as a community informant, passing on intelligence to the military about neighbors she suspected to be Boko Haram members. When she learned of Elder and his boys, she was impressed with their initiative and decided to sign up. She was twenty-four at the time. Fatima said that we wouldn't have been able to sit in Elder's living room talking as we were had it not been for the vigilantes. Her duties were few—frisking women coming into crowded public events, like religious festivals, and apprehending female suspects in their homes—but dangerous, since she didn't carry any weapons and there had been a rash of female suicide bombers in Maiduguri. One out of every five suicide bombings Boko Haram had recently staged or inspired had been executed by children, usually young girls. She was scared when she first started, Elder told me. But now, Fatima said with an easy swagger, she wasn't afraid at all.

According to the precepts of Islam, Elder and his boys couldn't enter the homes of women they did not know, even if they were suspected terrorists. That became Fatima's job. She surveyed the houses before approaching and then entered the compounds, armed with only a description of the woman she was arresting. "We came for you; you have to follow me," she told them, insisting even when they denied belonging to the group. Eventually, most of the women covered themselves and agreed to leave; they knew men with weapons were waiting outside. She never went to a house alone. The women often knew who she was, or they soon realized when they recognized the CJTF emblem Fatima wore. She sometimes went out on patrol with the vigilantes in the late hours of the night.

It was harder to do this work as a woman, she admitted. She felt more vulnerable if something were to go wrong. Her family in her home village Gamboru Ngala, outside Maiduguri, wanted her to stop. "But I have no option," she said.

After Fatima left, Elder stretched his legs on the carpeted floor of his living room to have lunch. The vigilantes were now using Italian-made rifles. He pulled one out from under his couch, along with a long magazine of bullets. He displayed them on the floor, and then, smirking, showed me cell phone photos of him in sunglasses with the gun wrapped around him. Children ran in and out of the house. He was happy. There were twenty-five children currently staying at his compound. "Some of them I don't even know their parents," he said. No matter. He would take care of them for as long as needed.

When he got home at night, in the little free time he had to himself, Elder thought about the future, and wondered when things would return to the way they had been before: businesses thriving, children going to school. He wondered if things would be better for his own children.

The Nigerian army, considerably aided by troops from neighboring Chad, had reclaimed most of the towns and villages Boko Haram had once occupied, and it had rescued hundreds of women and children from terrorist camps. Elder thought that soldiers stationed in and around Maiduguri appeared to be better armed under the anti-corruption drive of President Muhammadu Buhari, who was elected in May 2015. They seemed willing to go raid Boko Haram hideouts, instead of waiting to poorly defend themselves and civilians from attacks. But Boko Haram had recently assassinated a CJTF commander right outside of his home. Families who once had full houses in Chibok were now living packed together in single rooms in Maiduguri, where refugees from the countryside continued to come. More than 2 million people had left their homes. Farms had gone fallow, and trade had slowed.

We left his house. As we passed through the streets, we saw residents had tied barricades of bright rope across several of the narrow, pale sanded streets to prevent suicide bombers from getting too close to the area mosque. After they checked your car, they lowered the rope and let you pass. But people were out on the streets, walking, selling, talking, laughing. Children in purple school uniforms were playing and shrieking. Drying laundry hung on gates and fences.

Things crept toward what they were before. In January 2016, I met Rebecca on a hot afternoon in Abuja at Unity Park, the site of so many protests that demanded the government find the schoolgirls. Now the vast, grassy field was empty and quiet, the protestors forced to return to their own lives when the girls remained missing. We sat on a smooth slab of rock under a voluminous tree, drinking sodas a street vendor came by to sell us. Now twenty-one, Rebecca had discovered Shakespeare: Her favorite play was *Othello*. She constantly listened to the gospel music of Nigerian singer Solomon Lange. Emmanuel and his wife had five young children and she shared a room with them. They were a distraction, and a relief. The three boys made her laugh, and they all traded stories and jokes. "I'm able to forget everything when I am with them," Rebecca said. It had been a year and a half since she had left home; her parents wouldn't let her return because it was unsafe. Her three younger brothers called her and asked her when she would return. They were stuck in the house, unable to attend school. Almost 2 million children in Borno State were out of school because of the war. "I tell them, 'Very soon I will be back there,'" she said.

Most of her friends never came back. She knew she was

one of the lucky ones, the ones who got away when their country failed to protect them. She was supposed to be happy. More and more, she was. "My father," she laughed ruefully. "They tell him to leave that place and come here to Abuja. But he said no, he can't leave his land. He said Boko Haram will follow us to any part of Nigeria anyway, better to stay in our home." She thought about her parents all the time. There was no cell phone coverage near her house because Boko Haram had destroyed many of the towers in the region, and she could no longer talk to her parents and siblings whenever she wanted. Her father called her when he could, but it was not often enough. The last time he called, he told her about an attack in town. Suicide bombers had killed thirteen people in the market. She couldn't sleep that night.

Several months later, something unexpected happened. Rebecca learned of the return of twenty-two of her schoolmates. One girl named Amina was found wandering through Sambisa Forest with her infant child in May, and then Boko Haram released another twenty-one girls in October in a deal brokered by the Swiss government and the International Red Cross. Observers suspected the Nigerian government had paid a ransom to the terrorists or traded detained Boko Haram leaders for the girls, but the government denied the claims.

Rebecca was elated to hear her classmates had come back, if a little fearful to know what they had experienced in captivity. "I'm very, very happy," she said. God was looking out for them again. She had tried to reach the girls, but the government was keeping them cloistered in a rehabilitation center in the capital. "By the grace of God, more will come out," Rebecca predicted. In May 2017, as this book was going to press, Boko Haram released 82 more schoolgirls in exchange for the government's release of as many as six suspected members of the militant group. As many as 9,000 girls and women had been abducted by Boko Haram over the years to be their sex slaves, their cooks, and their suicide bombers. The militants tore into homes to kidnap girls, throwing a few naira to their parents for the "bride price."

Rebecca's parents agreed to let her visit home at the end of 2016. She was overjoyed to be with her family, absorbing their voices and smells, memorizing the ways their faces and bodies had shifted. But her trip lasted just six days because it was still too dangerous to be there. Some nights her parents and brothers slept in the bush with other people from her area if they heard rumors of a raid coming their way. It wasn't a way to live, but it's what they had to do now. Rebecca couldn't get rid of the feeling that the militants could come to Abuja to take her again. Her hand still ached from the jump that night. But she was doing what she had to do now, too. She had graduated from high school and was going to apply to university. "God gave me the opportunity to think about my future, so I can't let them stop me from going back to school," she said. She gave her head a final shake, and smiled. She had made up her mind.

By 2016, Elder was an "executive at the state level" for the CJTF, a title he wore proudly. He managed its finances and coordinated all the sectors of the force, a move that only increased the pressures on him, though he was in battle less often. It pained Elder that the office he rented for sector five had gone to waste. The man who took his place never went there.

When he was not at the auditor's office, he took pleasure in taking his children to school and keeping up his home. But dangers persisted. Three militants had ridden motorbikes in front of the house where his third wife lived, near the local headquarters of the Central Bank of Nigeria. They saw his wife in the road, not knowing it was his wife, and asked her where Elder lived. She lied and told them he didn't live around there, giving them another location. The vice chairman of sector nine had recently been at home with his family when a woman came to his house. She called him outside, and when he stepped out of his home, she blew them both up with explosives she was carrying.

More Boko Haram members had showed up at Elder's family compound. "They've been targeting my house for a long time," he said. It was in the evening, and Elder was not at home. A woman who lived nearby was sitting at the gate to the compound. When she saw two young men wander toward her, she thought that they could be *almajiri*, students at the nearby madrassas who begged for money or food. She offered them food but they refused. She asked if they wanted to see someone living inside the house. They said no. Another neighbor was watching them and walked over to the group. He wanted to know who the boys were. He got close to them, eyeing them carefully, and noticed that their clothes appeared to be bulging. He shouted, "These people are carrying bombs!" The woman started screaming. The young men quickly ran away. Before Elder arrived at the scene, his own boys had already surrounded his home. Elder assumed his mask of bravado: He claimed he hadn't been worried, and that his family had not been afraid. It was easier to cope with the unknowns, and the fear, that way. His neighbors had told him to move his family, to take heed of the warnings from Boko Haram and protect themselves. They complained when he traveled—both his family and his neighbors were left vulnerable. "At times I cannot sleep at all," his wife Hamsutu said. "And we are always afraid they will bring back his body." Elder would not listen.

When more of the Chibok girls came home, Elder was in the most tolerant mood I had ever seen him. In retrospect, he gave some credit to the military for not striking Boko Haram heedlessly since the militants could have killed the girls during an operation. "The military had done what they could do with the capacity they had at that time," he said. And if the government had indeed negotiated with the terrorists, he didn't mind. In every conflict, he had realized, there must be dialogue along with the fighting. Tens of thousands of people had been killed so far because of this war. Over 25,000 people had died in Borno State alone. "We are ready to accept peace," he told me. "You cannot end war with war." He didn't want to do this forever. He wanted to have his own farm, grow peaches and raise chickens. Ride his tractor through the mango and lemon trees.

4

SOMALIA

The Last Two Stadiums in Mogadishu

WHEN AISHA was 16, a man knocked on the front door of her home one evening. Her mother wasn't at home, so her older brother Mohamed answered the door. The man asked him the whereabouts of his sister. Mohamed said that she was at home, and the man asked him to get her. Mohamed called for her, and Aisha came to the door. Once the man saw her, he told Mohamed to go back inside. "Come, we need you," he said to Aisha. Mohamed yelled that she was not going anywhere. He grabbed Aisha's hand and slammed the door closed.

The man was undeterred. He came to a window and said he needed to talk to Aisha. He pounded on the closed window and shouted for her to join him outside. "Please come outside, we want to tell you something," he said through the glass. "Open the window." She shouted that she would not. The man left. She tried to sleep that night but had trouble closing her eyes and calming down. She was afraid he would return. Aisha had practice early the next morning and went to the court. After it was over, she got home safely and didn't see the man from that night again. She forced herself to keep her mind on basketball, as always. She just hoped unknown men stayed away from her home. "I don't know what the future will hold," she mused. "There could be more things like this, I don't know."

Aisha's mother was often out of town in Somaliland, to do business and to see her sick aunt. She left her daughter in the care of Aisha's half sister when she traveled. But the security in Aisha's sister's neighborhood was getting worse. My driver was nervous going there and told my friend Hana, a young Somali filmmaker, and me that we would either have to finish within a few minutes, or that he would leave and then pick us up when we were ready to go. Hana was working on a documentary on women's basketball in Somalia. She lived in Abu Dhabi with her parents and siblings, and had spent time in Mogadishu filming the players. Aisha's neighbors watched us carefully as we disembarked from the truck and walked into her house. Before I could deliberate on whether it seemed secure enough to remain behind without transportation, Hana had told them to go. We were in a private house and that would keep us safe, she reasoned.

We walked into a muddy courtyard—it had rained all night—and then onto the porch of a bright blue house, where Aisha's aunt and female cousins were combing and braiding their hair, pulling on blouses and headscarves, drinking tea. A faint, melodic call to prayer came from somewhere outside the gate. The girls and women looked at us with silent curiosity as we followed Aisha. The room where Aisha had been sleeping was through the porch. Dim and drowsy, the room had one window with half-open blue shutters; a crookedly hung drape blew over it from a faint breeze. Two mattresses with the sheets pushed aside were on the floor, and the three of us settled on top of them. A worn rug lay under the beds and a low wooden table stood in the corner near the door.

The older Aisha became, the more she argued with her relatives. She had recently fought with her brother-in-law. "In the years before the civil war, women used to go without the hijab and represent Somalia internationally while not wearing almost anything," Aisha told him. "We shouldn't say now that Islam doesn't let us play." Her mother, Warsan, also swam competitively before the war, and went around in her bathing suit and without covering her hair at all. Aisha thought it was good Somalis were more in tune with their religion now—in her mother's day, people didn't really know much about Islam, she thought—but she didn't think anyone should control how women carried themselves. If she wanted to uncover her hair, she uncovered it. She had seen girls walk around with their heads bare. "I prefer that people should do whatever they want," she said. "It should be their choice, not someone forcing them or telling them what to do. As long as you have that connection with God." It didn't make sense that God would care about girls playing basketball if they tried to be faithful and good.

She thought of herself as devoted to Islam. She had memorized the entire Koran, and her uncle had a library of Islamic books, most of which she had read. She was even helping teach a friend the Koran at that moment. ("If you don't memorize the Koran and if you don't stay with your religion, you will be lost," Aisha told her girlfriend.) "Praying and reading the Koran and going through these books that my uncle has gives me the feeling of being connected to God. It gives me the feeling that, on Judgment Day, I will not be judged because I missed my prayer or anything else, inshallah," she explained. Freedom to her meant being able to do whatever she wanted, as long as it wasn't morally wrong or what God had explicitly said not to do. She wanted to go to heaven, and so she tried to follow the Prophet. She covered her hair and wore long pants during practice and games. But her God wouldn't want her to stop playing. Warsan drove her to practice whenever possible, and she came to her games when she could. Aisha loved women like her mother and her coach Nasro for their fearlessness.

Nasro started playing basketball in the south of Somalia, in a city called Baidoa, where she grew up. She learned to play in school, where she also ran track. When she was still a teenager, she came to Mogadishu to play for teams in the city. Her team was called Jeenyo, one of the best in those days. She walked around in basketball shorts with her hair uncovered, and was respected. "It was peaceful in our time," Nasro said. "We had all the freedom. We used to walk from our houses to the basketball court wearing trousers and Afros. And then we would go home around midnight still wearing whatever we wore to the court." No one really cared. Nasro wasn't used to the way things were now for women. She liked to wear glittery, bright headscarves and gold jewelry, and there were parts of the city where she could no longer wear them openly. She didn't have a car, so she would be a target walking through those quarters. She would have to put on a niqab to hide her face, and so she carried the black fabric around in her bag, just in case.

"Now people take religion as everything. They tell you to cover yourself, force it on you," Nasro said. They didn't teach sports in school to girls anymore, so her fourteen-year-old daughter gathered all her female and male friends and classmates who were interested in basketball, and Nasro taught them privately. On Saturdays, she took them to the court to practice. Nasro had fair skin and mirthful eyes. She wore glasses with black-and-hot-pink frames and her teeth were a gleaming white with several gold caps. She was now in her late forties and as sprightly as ever.

During the fighting, Nasro left for the United Arab Emirates. When she returned to Somalia in 2012, she got involved again with women's basketball, which was struggling. "I came back and took about thirty girls and trained them," she said. "Those are some of the girls you see on the court today." But she soon became frustrated that the head of the basketball federation was foiling the efforts of the girls' teams to hold practices and games at the court. She had to get a hold of donations herself for the girls: uniforms, balls, shoes. The federation was corrupt, she knew, and mostly concerned with pocketing any money that came the athletes' way.

It was not easy to protect the girls. "A lot of girls want to play but they're scared. They will play, but they're still scared. A lot of people will talk bad about you, starting from your neighbors. If you don't wear the hijab, people will start talking on the street, and you always have to be alert because at the court you don't know who is who, who could kill you because you're wearing trousers," Nasro said. "And the federation doesn't like girls to play. They don't want to mess with al-Shabaab so they put up obstacles to the girls forming teams."

And so, as much as Aisha loved her country, she thought of leaving all the time. A lot of other young people she knew thought of it. The promise of freedom and riches outside of Somalia's borders was much too seductive and heady. "If I get a chance, I would leave," she said. She would get into one of those overcrowded, rickety boats and take her chances on the sea. Aisha had no doubts. She would go far away from this place until it somehow became better, felt safe again. She wasn't planning to go back to school or go to college; that wasn't for her. So what was left for her here? As brave as she was, she was afraid of dying. There was still so much to do. "I can't act like I'm weak," she went on. "My weakness puts me in more danger. So I need to act strong and tough. I tell them I am going to do whatever I want." She asked if I would take her back to America in my suitcase, an impish smile crawling up her face.

• • •

Only two stadiums still stood in Mogadishu after the war. Efforts to reconstruct others had lagged and then stopped. Mogadishu Stadium, where athletes had competed in swimming, soccer, handball, basketball, and volleyball, had been one of the largest stadiums in all of East Africa. There had been swimming pools and other amenities for athletes in the complex. African Union soldiers had since taken it over, installing their operations in the once-resplendent facility. But, as ever, Somalis had found their own solutions when the stadiums failed to materialize. People played sports on the streets, in lots and fields, and on the beach, and they started building small open-air courts themselves. Sometimes the government would lay turf in the makeshift courts, but the sports ministry didn't have much of a budget. In 2010, it provided, for a time, security for practices and games it deemed risky for participants and fans, especially in women's basketball. But now many of the men's national teams, like in soccer and basketball, traveled through the continent to compete. The national women's basketball team hadn't left the country since the Pan Arab Games in Qatar in 2011, when they placed fourth out of twenty-two countries. It was the only tournament the women's team had played since the civil war began in 1991. The sports ministry blamed the team's lack of travel on the basketball federation, which managed both the men's and women's club teams.

The men's basketball teams had uniforms and gear, regular games and practices, and space to play. The

women's teams had none of that. And the basketball federation often clashed with the women's teams' coaches.
When the coaches learned of opportunities to take their
players to international tournaments, the federation usually blocked their attempts to participate. Basketball was
one of the oldest and most popular sports among women
in Somalia, and the women's national team used to be
one of the best in the region. Many of its past stars recruited and trained young girls in the hopes that a new,
active national team would solidify. But even in parts of
the country where al-Shabaab was not in charge, their
influence had seeped through society, circumscribing the
roles of girls and women and limiting their choices.
"Families are putting a lot of pressure on girls," Osman
Aden Dhubow, the deputy sports minister, told me in
his office. "You can't do this, you can't dress like this,
you can't play. Before, girls could play freely, dress how
they wanted, they had their training facilities, they had
finances. They don't have that now. They don't have the
right coaches. Everything is at the wrong time."

I asked the ministry officials, both men, when the
women's basketball teams would next have a game. It
took them several long minutes to figure out when the
girls would be playing. The girls had so many restraints:
the men's and women's teams shared the few courts, and
the men's teams evidently had priority; some of the girls
played other sports and their coaches wouldn't allow them
to leave practice for basketball; and there weren't enough
female referees, and that complicated putting on women's
games. In other words, very few people seemed to care if

the girls had the chance to play basketball or not. At that moment, we heard two loud booms that sounded like explosions or mortar fire. Startled, I stopped in the middle of asking my next question. "Don't worry," Ifrah, my interpreter, said. They were so used to explosions, like the rest of Mogadishu, that bombs and gunshots had faded into everyday background noise. She motioned for me to continue talking.

There were rumors that the Olympic Committee was nervous about sending girls to compete abroad because of threats from al-Shabaab. "We have to avoid as much as we can the risks," Duran Ahmed Farah, the president of the Somali Olympic Committee, said vaguely. "Culturally, it's not easy for girls to play sports outside. You cannot find a lot of girls playing sports at the moment because there are no suitable facilities in the country—not only in Mogadishu, but everywhere. The boys can play football on the road, on the streets, but it doesn't look good to a community if girls are playing sports outside." He echoed the sports ministry's stance about how the government was trying to build facilities where girls could play safely. But this supposed duty to protect girls' modesty by keeping them inside was part of the problem itself, one I hadn't seen in almost any other African country where I had spent time, even in ones with mostly Muslim populations, like Senegal, which was generally more moderate in its religious beliefs and practices.

Somalia had wanted to compete in the Olympics in Rio de Janeiro that year, but none of its athletes had qualified, so it was tradition for countries in that position to bring its best male and female athletes. It had been difficult to find a girl, Farah said, but they would likely bring a track-and-field athlete. It was less controversial than bringing a girl who played a contact sport.

There was something about a group of girls, urgently devoted to scoring a goal, or making a basket, through any means necessary, scuffling, pushing, and pulling, that deeply offended men who couldn't stand to see women with both strength and agency The sight of a girl who could fight and defend and force herself into where she needed to be was frightening. It meant that she had a mind of her own that no man could touch, or ever hope to control. In a place with fragile law and order, those who were targeted were the most vulnerable. In a country like Somalia, those people were its women, but only due to the reach of extremism. Because women were the reason the fabric of the country had barely stayed intact, as their men fought in battle, their sons died in the bloodshed, and their homes fell into ruin.

Much of the archives and photos of the national women's basketball team in the 1970s and 1980s had been lost. The war had destroyed museums and galleries and libraries and most other places where Somali stories had been kept and nourished. When asked how they could make playing the sport safer for girls, government officials said there were bigger issues to deal with, like education and health. There were now hundreds of girls and women playing basketball, but the interests of girls just didn't rank as high.

·   ·   ·

In 2016, Aisha joined the team OFC. She also became the captain. Her coach, Mulki Nur, was quiet and unassuming and melted into the background, except when she was on the court. Her loose, muted jilbabs couldn't hide her height and strong build, and the way she grabbed the ball when she needed to. Mulki played for the national women's basketball team in the 1980s. It was the team's heyday. She was too young to stop when she did, at twenty-five, but war didn't care about those things. They played at the Pan Arab Games, and traveled to Iraq, Jordan, and Morocco. "All I wanted was to play basketball around the world," she told me, her plain face brightening. "I was happy, and I was proud of what I was doing." The country was safe then, and Somalis had a real government. She went with her friends anywhere in the city she wanted, at any time. But it had become so dangerous that she left the country in 2008 with the hopes of reaching Europe. "I was being chased by the militants," she said. She was helping coach girls at the time. She started receiving calls through the day, every day, from men who threatened to kill her if she continued coaching. "The security level then was very bad," she said. "And it would have been easy for them to get to me." Within days, she left Somalia.

Mulki crossed to Ethiopia and made her way to Sudan, intending to go on to Libya and then over the Mediterranean Sea to Europe. The plan was to get there and then find a way to bring her children. But she was caught in Sudan and deported to Ethiopia. Then Ethiopia sent her back home to Mogadishu. She had ten children, five girls and five boys. When she left Somalia, she had to leave them behind with her husband. "I believe that women should be free," she said. "They should have their full freedom. Although it is very dangerous for girls to play now, we still continue playing basketball."

They did keep playing, Aisha most of all. Not long before she joined Mulki's team, Aisha and a friend were on a bus one evening headed to the court for practice. They weren't wearing niqabs, the dark enveloping robes that fell to the ground and shielded your face. Many of the girls on the team wore them when they entered and left the court to avoid people recognizing them as members of the teams. Nasro had posted photos of Aisha and the others at a recent game on Facebook, and anyone could see they belonged to the league. But Aisha refused to wear one. "I don't care; I just show my face," she said. She and her friend were seated in the last row of the bus. A man sitting near them stuck out his phone; on it was a Facebook photo from the game. "Is this you? Is this you?" he demanded. The girls said they were not the ones in the photos. The man said that if they did not stop playing, he would kill them. He held up a gun and pointed it at the two girls.

Aisha could see the face of the man holding the gun; there was nothing hiding it. He was wearing a white shirt and black pants. He looked normal, like any man you could meet on the street. When he pointed the gun at them, the bus driver shouted, "What's happening? Why are you pointing a gun at these girls?" The man said it was none of his business. He fired his gun above the girls' heads, hitting the side of the bus, and said he wanted to get off. When the vehicle stopped, he told Aisha and her friend to leave with him. Aisha refused, but her friend was standing up to go. "I held her hand and said to her, 'If you get off, he will take you and kill you. Let's stay here with the passengers. Let him kill us in front of everyone," Aisha recalled. Aisha was shocked and sweating, but she almost felt numb. "It was not my first time with the militants, and I was kind of getting used to it," she said. She had no other option. Her mother had begged her to stop playing basketball, or to join their relatives living elsewhere in East Africa. Aisha didn't want her mother to worry, but she wasn't going to do either of those things just yet.

Everyone got off the bus. Soldiers on the street saw the man with the gun and came to apprehend him. Aisha and her friend walked to the court in silence, and got ready for practice.

As 2016 went on, Aisha was having problems with the basketball federation. It had thwarted the girls' chance to go to a tournament in the United Arab Emirates, and Aisha had expressed her disapproval in a local interview. She told the reporter that it wasn't fair and that women's sports deserved more attention. "Some people in the federation do want to improve women's basketball," she told me. "But others do not want any improvement for us. They just want us to keep playing by ourselves without participating in tournaments outside of the country." The federation had suspended her for playing at an event promoting women in sports without telling it first, but she had managed to get the decision overturned.

Aisha was realizing that basketball wasn't everything to her. "I want to both play basketball and sing," she said, a grand smile on her face. A local radio station held singing contests for kids in the area, and she liked to participate. She sang songs that told stories about her country. Her parents didn't like her interest in singing, though their disapproval had never mattered that much to her. Her mother, Warsan, was resigned: She said Aisha would take her own path. Aisha had just thrown a party for her friends at a hotel that became an illicit club at night. They had danced to Somali and American pop music, drank, ate cake, and she had held her boyfriend. Being at a club was risky; militants had targeted them with explosives in the past. But Aisha usually found a way to do what she wanted.

When she didn't have enough money for the bus to the court, she worked hard to pull it together, asking her neighbors for help or calling her teammates to see if anyone could pick her up. "I go beyond everything just to get to the court," Aisha said. "I didn't have the right shoes, or clothes, anything, when I first started playing." Nasro had helped her get all the equipment she needed, and she was grateful. Aisha had come too far to give it all up now. Her love of basketball made her "not see anything negative," she went on. "When you have the kind of love and passion I have for basketball, everything else is kind of blurry. They don't really matter. That's how I overcame those things I went through."

One afternoon in April 2016, I headed to Wiish Stadium, a towering basketball court in the Banaadir quarter, past the city's corniche, where the brick wall barely kept the ocean at bay. Children, families, and couples gathered at the wall's edge and jumped back when the waves leaped over. At the stadium, I met a stout man with a salt-and-pepper beard named Abdulkadir Moalin, who helped run the basketball federation. After we sat down on a concrete bleacher, he tried to explain why the girls never went anywhere to compete. The members of the federation didn't get paid, he said, and their work was on a voluntary basis. So they had to recruit sponsors that paid for the teams' travel. It was a false impression, he went on, that all the sponsorship money seemed to go to the men. "Different people, different opinions," he said dismissively, shrugging. "There are no resources at all!" He became agitated. "How many women presidents have you had?" he asked suddenly, referring to the United States. Hana had arranged for several of the girls to enter a tournament in Abu Dhabi the previous year. Nasro had been excited and on board. But when Hana and Nasro brought the proposal to the federation, they balked. Now Moalin told me that a lack of funds and holding a Somali passport had kept the girls from traveling.

I grew tired of talking with him and began watching the game, which had just started. The two teams were energetic and scrappy, with a mix of experienced and novice players. They were clearly enjoying themselves. Aisha was pugilistic, constantly thinking and scheming. Her teammate, a short girl with dark skin and a slight build, kept stealing the ball to take shot after shot. Despite missing nearly all of them, her face stayed in a wide grin. When the other team gained the chance to take a three-point shot, she went over to the shooter and congratulated her, beaming, after the player made the basket. The audience was mostly made up of men and boys—many were relatives or friends of the players—and some women. The court was painted in a faded pale blue, peach, and green, and the girls' bright jerseys in orange and yellow glowed against the sky. Next door stood a cream mansion edged by bushy green trees. It was pockmarked with bullet holes.

The manager of my hotel was a Somali-Canadian woman in her midtwenties named Ayaan, who had moved to Mogadishu a few years earlier. She had grown up in Canada, but had realized that she liked being immersed in Somali culture and being a part of her country's perpetual struggle for progress. Life had a purpose, more meaning, for her here. Her cousin was Ifrah, my interpreter, who had asked me to smuggle in the tequila. Ifrah showed up late to our first meeting. She usually didn't venture outside during the daytime because of the heat, she said. Most of her friends didn't either. She had been out late the previous night, drinking and smoking pot with friends on the beach. I was shocked. She laughed. Ifrah always wore a headscarf, but her makeup was seductive and she posted unveiled photos of herself on Instagram. She had grown up in Nairobi and had lived wildly there—partying, drinking, doing drugs—and her concerned mother had decided to send her to live with relatives in Mogadishu to turn her into a well-behaved woman.

A lot of Somali parents did the same thing with their misbehaving, young adult children, and the overgrown kids managed to re-create in Mogadishu the libertine environment they had left behind. Ifrah had gotten pregnant not long after she moved; she was no longer dating her child's father. Some of the children sent to Mogadishu were even in their thirties, like a married father who was an alcoholic and whose parents had forced him to move to Mogadishu to rehabilitate himself among family. Instead he drank more than ever, as his wife and children remained behind in England. The duty Somali children felt to their parents was so strong that even a grown man with his own family would obey the wishes of his parents, turn over his passport to them, and carry out his penance in a place foreign to him.

Ifrah had been caught drinking by the police too many nights to remember. Most of the time, if a policeman stumbled upon her and a group of friends drinking on the beach, they gave him a bottle of liquor and he left them alone. But if she was drunk and argued with the officer, he would put her in a holding cell in jail overnight, which had happened at least half a dozen times. It wasn't a big deal to them; they avoided al-Shabaab by partying at night (no attacks ever happened at night, according to their reasoning), and so the corrupt, ineffectual police weren't a concern. The day for them began late, since few of the people in Ifrah's circle actually worked, with dinner at a restaurant and then drinks in a hotel room they rented. As the night expanded into dawn, they made their way to the beach. They were part of a diaspora that was moving "back" to Somalia, whose members were called repatriates, or repats. Never mind that most repats had not grown up, or even been born, in Somalia; they had come to the country to live and work and join in the rebuilding of the nation. If they weren't Somalis who had returned after leaving during the fighting, they were sons and daughters of parents who kept Somalia alive in houses thousands of miles away from their homeland.

There was tension between the Somalis who had stayed behind and the ones who had returned. Somalis from the diaspora got better jobs, had more money to spend, and generally led lives of more luxury and privilege. It wasn't unusual to hear a Somali-Canadian at a restaurant in Mogadishu asking if the meat was organic. Still, young people would always have things in common: wanting to decide their futures for themselves, wanting to have fun, wanting to be free.

One night, Hana took me to another hotel with a courtyard that turned into a nightclub in the late hours. At close to midnight, she showed up at my hotel in a carful of friends, young Somalis who had been recently deported back to Mogadishu from Saudi Arabia because of a change in immigration rules in that country. The courtyard was dark and thrumming with people. They were dancing to American hip-hop and Somali pop; people were smoking hookah and flirting over lit-up smartphones; and the bartender even told me he had a "white alcohol" if I was interested, but I wasn't going to drink anything mysteriously called white alcohol, so I opted for hookah and watermelon juice. Occasionally

Hana or I tried to take a photo of the place, but the people around us gave us suspicious looks; they didn't want to be identified as being there. We danced and talked until I told Hana that I needed to get back to my hotel. I was worried about being at a place that was so vulnerable to a sudden attack, even though no one else seemed to be. When I left, the young, and some not so young, repat and local Somalis were still dancing and smoking with abandon.

I had been a repat, too, when I moved to Lagos in 2012 and found myself in a scene of Nigerians who had grown up or went to school in the West, and then had moved to the country to make money, fall in love, and be, in many different senses, home. The first man I dated in Lagos had grown up in the city and gone to the American School, and then left to attend college and work for a few years in the United States before coming back to join his father's oil and gas company. He and his adult brothers lived in his parents' mansion, gaudily decorated in the nouveau riche Nigerian way, and he drove around town in a shiny black SUV he shared with one of his brothers. I loved his ability to switch between an American accent and flawless Nigerian pidgin—that, to me, was the sign of a perfectly adjusted and streetwise repat. A lot of young repats lived in their parents' homes because the city was so expensive; landlords usually required two years' worth of rent up front. I alternated between renting a room at a place called the African Artists' Foundation, which housed visiting artists, writers, and scholars in a sprawling house filled with West African art, and subletting guest rooms in friends of friends' apartments.

Lagos was the love of our lives and the bane of our existences. We danced at a rotating set of nightclubs; gathered at art exhibit openings and literary readings; saw each other at the same birthdays, weddings, and christenings; and went to surprisingly nice beaches not far outside of the city. We also overpaid for the same imported food and drinks, overpaid for the same generators because there was little electricity, and overpaid for the same apartments and houses because of those electricity problems. But Lagos's energy was addictive. Despite how much it could frustrate you, its hustle and creativity were stimulating. People did not like to beg. You would complain often there; you would also accomplish some of your finest work.

Public services were lacking in Lagos, so its inhabitants came up with innovative ways to survive. Even in prosperous gated communities, residents bought generators for electricity, dug boreholes for water, and hired guards for security. Yinka Marinho, who used to head the Lagos government's waterways agency, once told me, "We have the most expensive slums in the world. We're paying a lot for nothing; no running water, no power." I didn't mind much, even when the city, bereft of gutters, sank under the rain and roads disappeared. We pulled up our trousers to wade through the water, as cars slowed to a near halt to tentatively plow through rapidly forming lakes.

But when I was with friends late at night driving and blasting music on Third Mainland Bridge, the path over Lagos Lagoon that was the second-longest bridge in

Africa, as we headed to a club or house party, everything was right with the world. I was doing what I was supposed to be doing, with the people I was supposed to be doing it, in the best city in the world. It was how I knew what young Somalis, freshly returned from abroad, must be feeling as they smoked up on the beach, drank illegal alcohol, and tried to create their country all over again.

Late one weekday afternoon in May 2016, in her shared bedroom at her sister's house, Aisha was wearing a long blue and white floral skirt, a pale blouse, and a dark floral print headscarf. She was wearing light makeup: tinted lip gloss, kohl, and blush. She looked stunning sitting on her mattress, the embodiment of a feminine Somali woman, one who was giggling about her boyfriend and constantly checking her phone. She then stood up and walked to the opposite side of the room to rummage through a red suitcase lying open on the table. Aisha stripped off nearly everything she was wearing, the skirt, the blouse, and the headscarf, and replaced them with a red cotton tank top and a sky-blue jersey with the number ten on the back. (She had already been wearing the matching blue track pants under her skirt.) She retied the headscarf around her head, this time knotting it firmly in the back, like a cloth-covered bun, instead of letting it secure under her chin and drape around her shoulders in the traditional way. Next, she pulled on a floor-length, red-and-black-striped cotton skirt over her pants. She shrugged into a mustard yellow jilbab, which had an opening just for her face and fell almost to her knees over the headscarf and jersey. She was ready to play ball.

She got into the car with me and Hana, and we drove through the city to an indoor basketball court at the end of a labyrinthine market in the quarter Hamar Weyne. People filled the slender streets as they crowded among the stalls, navigated around the traffic, and transported livestock and cargo on battered carts. People gathered on the sidewalks and in the roads to talk and trade.

Hana stuck her bulky camera out the window, reassuring the driver and me that she had walked around the market on her last trip with a video camera and nothing had happened. Still, our driver said, she could scare people because she was holding an object in a pose that was not immediately recognizable; she could be a potential grenade thrower. Hana reluctantly put her camera back on her lap.

Outside the indoor court was another court, enclosed by peeling pink cement walls. Within the walls, some men were sitting on the bleachers, low cement slabs in a graduated formation the length of the court. Soccer nets had been placed under the two basketball hoops. Aisha's teammates, girls and young women dressed like her, were scattered through the place, shooting hoops indoors, running on treadmills in the steamy exercise room in the back, and lounging on benches outside, gossiping and catching up. Although they weren't much safer here than anywhere else in Mogadishu, they were loud and carefree: This court was home. Strangers could walk in and wreak whatever terror they wanted; there was no security. But there seemed to be an invisible force inside those cement walls defying anyone from doing so.

One of the girls had an American accent. Her name was Khadro. She was visiting from New York and had come to stay with her grandmother for the summer. She played basketball at home, and an uncle in Mogadishu had suggested that she join one of the local teams while she was in town. She was amazed, she told me, at the girls who played amid all the conservative morals they were supposed to uphold. Her cousin had come with her to watch the practice.

Aisha roamed assertively around the grounds, and her voice rose and landed on top of the others.

"Heegan is no joke," Khadro's cousin said, referring to a team that rivaled Aisha's team, OFC. "Heegan is powerful, huh?"

"Heegan is the best team," he went on. "They actually own this court."

"OFC is getting better. It *is* better," Aisha countered.

"I like the shirt that you're wearing," he said, smiling appreciatively at her blue jersey.

"Heegan is taking everything," he went on observing. "It's the best in football, handball, all of the sports."

Aisha's voice rose to a shriek.

"The Heegan football team is not that great. They're in fourth place!" she yelled. "OFC is the number one team! This ground belongs to me!"

The other girls laughed. Aisha was haughty and combative, but comically so. It was hard not to be charmed by the fierceness coming from such a slight person.

Aisha became bored with the conversation and went inside. She grabbed the ball and started dribbling, drawing some of the other girls into an impromptu game. Before long, her shouts could be heard through the court.

For so many of Aisha's teammates, and girls on other teams, basketball invited constant danger. Her former teammate Amaal, who was eighteen and had serious eyes, began playing basketball in 2009. Being on the court made Amaal more social than she had ever been, as she met new girls, made friends, and created a whole other home. "I used to be at the house doing nothing; I never had any friends," Amaal said. "Basketball lets me know more about myself. It's changed me. I'm around women who are passionate, who are my friends." She could spend the entire day just at the court. If she didn't have money for public transportation to practice, she would walk. Her family was poor and her parents couldn't find work, but her father would ask his friends for money so that Amaal could get to the court and buy proper shoes and gear.

Amaal's friend Faiza had been the one to get her to pick up a ball. Faiza was brimming with life and well liked. The day before a game Amaal and Faiza were playing, Faiza had a friend over to her home for lunch. That evening, after the friend had left, al-Shabaab militants arrived at her house. They took her to an empty lot far from her home and, hours later, left her body there. The men didn't just kill her. They tortured her, cutting her body and face with shards of glass, shaving her head, leaving marks all over her. She was bruised, torn to bits, thrown away as if there weren't people who loved her. Amaal was completely shaken. "When I heard that one of my friends was killed for loving basketball, it made me really scared for my life," she said.

Amaal realized the magnitude of what she was doing when she went to the court. "You put your life in danger in this country because of the thing that you love," she said. After the murder, she was depressed for months. She would tell herself, unconvincingly, that she had to move on with her life. But she was having dreams about Faiza. And, like with Aisha, the calls soon started. Unfamiliar, menacing voices telling her to stop playing. They called all the time. Once, when she was having dinner with her family, she put the caller on speaker for them to hear. They called her a Christian, as if Amaal had renounced her own faith by playing basketball as a woman. They said she worked for the Christians, who had brainwashed her. "We know you've left Islam," they said. "We're going to kill you. We're going to cut off your head." She told them that she wasn't a Christian, and that she played basketball for herself. "Where are the Christians in Somalia?" she asked. "This is for my own life." They denounced the fact that she wore pants during games and said that she was trying to be a man. They told her she wouldn't go to heaven. "That's funny," she said to one. "You guys are killing people and you think you're going to heaven?"

A few years later, Amaal met Nasro, who told her that she was getting together girls who were good at basketball and had a passion for it. She wanted Amaal to join them, and she introduced Amaal to a leading women's team called Horseed. The coach put her on the junior team. Amaal forced herself to go to the first practice even though she was apprehensive about her safety. She didn't want to die for this, only for this, when she knew what she was doing wasn't wrong. "It made me stronger," Amaal recalled. Every morning she went to the gym to work out, and then she met up with Nasro's group in the afternoon. She hid that she played basketball from most people, including her relatives and friends, because she didn't know who she could trust, who was on her side. She was still piecing back together her life after it dissolved into debris during the Ethiopian military occupation. Her family lost their house during the fighting and had to move with any possessions they could salvage into a refugee camp, where many of their neighbors were already setting up homes. But by May 2016, Amaal and her family had their own home again, renting two bedrooms and a bathroom in a house where each room opened onto a narrow courtyard.

And so Amaal felt determined. "I see it as something very powerful, to be young and a woman in a country that is not safe and has gone through a lot of war, and to have a dream and wear pants and a shirt and hold a basketball— there's nothing stronger to me," Amaal said. "To think about what I want for myself and to do it." It was needed, she believed, what she and Aisha and the other girls were doing, and Somalia would lose something important if they let the militants take the few things women had to themselves, the releases and the joys.

•   •   •

At the end of December 2016, Aisha traveled with her team to the northern city of Garowe, in the Puntland region, for Somalia's first nationwide women's basketball tournament. Aisha was so excited she couldn't stop talking in the days leading to the games; she had been looking forward to this for months. On the way to the airport in Mogadishu, she and the girls danced and sang Somali pop love songs in the minivan until a coach begged them to sit down. Teams were coming from all over the country to play. But just before Christmas Day, a group of influential clerics called the Somali Religious Council released a statement calling basketball "un-Islamic" and a "threat to their faith." The council's spokesman said that the sport could corrupt them. He warned girls like Aisha not to show their "body and beauty" for men to see. Although the council had preached against the radicalism of al-Shabaab, it mostly agreed with the terrorist group on the need to control the liberties of women.

Aisha was proudly wearing her electric yellow-and-black athletic shirt and pants, but she boarded the plane with trepidation. "I was afraid of what they were saying. All of my teammates were afraid," she said. She had seen statements from the clerics on Facebook encouraging people in Garowe to hurt them. They even promised to cut the girls' throats. But she was soon distracted by the delight of being on a plane, peering down through the clouds at her receding hometown, and then landing in a new place, less crazed and tense than Mogadishu. They arrived at the airport in the city Bosaso, and then piled in a van to drive almost 300 miles to Garowe. They kept singing, and they stuck their hands out of the car and screamed at people as they passed. The girls were staying in a hotel, where they met the members of the competing teams. "It was an amazing feeling. I was really happy to meet new girls from different regions," Aisha said "Playing with them was fun. If we won or lost, I was happy either way."

Some hidden part of her had always thought this was possible, to play a real tournament against girls from outside Mogadishu who had their own teams, but she had never really let herself believe it. Now it was all before her: the beautiful, expansive court with a pale-green ground that was theirs for the next week; the time they spent, day and night, only playing basketball; the happy, fascinating girls who were unafraid. In Garowe, there were no eyes watching, waiting to threaten her. She could be, for these fleeting days, whole, showing all sides of herself at once.

At the games, the raucous audience was full of women: young, older, holding babies, in jilbabs in an array of colors. An elderly woman yelled until her voice grew hoarse. It was the first basketball game for many of them, and they enthusiastically cheered both teams, refusing to pick a side. During the opening game, after the first half, the crowd rushed the court, thinking that it was already over.

In the end, the girls tried to satisfy the clerics who didn't want them on the court. The religious leaders had said the basketball players were naked, and being sinful, but the players decided to show them that they could be pious on the clerics' terms, and defiant. Security guards stood at the entrance to the stadium, frisking everyone who entered, but the girls also played wearing hijab, along with the usual long pants and shirts. Aisha didn't like wearing all that clothing to play; it was hot and uncomfortable under those layers, but she wouldn't let any man hurt her or her friends. If wearing a hijab on the court kept them safer during such an important moment, she would do it—this time.

Each night, after the day's games, she, her teammates, and her coach got together to dance and sing more love songs, jumping on the beds and screaming the words, to keep their energy high. After a series of challenging games, her team won second place. Aisha was more confident than ever in her playing, and she wanted to transfer to Horseed, the best team in the league. There was something rarefied about being at the tournament in Garowe, a feeling she wanted to hold on to as long as she could. For once, she didn't have to think about her family, or her boyfriend, or her neighbors, and what they would think of her choices. She was free.

Eunice and Bosco with their son Tadeo.

ACKNOWLEDGMENTS

First, a list of the books that helped inform my reporting: *The Wizard of the Nile* by Matthew Green, *Aboke Girls* by Els De Temmerman, *Boko Haram* by Virginia Comolli, and *Getting Somalia Wrong?* by Mary Harper.

To the subjects of this book: my eternal affection and gratitude. Thank you for letting me into your lives, and for allowing me to probe your memories over and over again, including the most traumatic ones. I also thank you for cooperating with my process, as I sought to corroborate those memories whenever it was possible.

Among the people and institutions I would like to thank for their kindness, generosity, guidance, and support are: Hana Mire, Jin Auh, Paul Whitlatch, Lauren Hummel, Victor Oloya, Theo Hollander, Brahim Ramadhane, Dame Ba, Abidine Maatalla, Lawan Abana, Ayuba Yamta, Hamza Idris, Mustapha Muhammed, Nike Lawrence,

ACKNOWLEDGMENTS

Anh-Thu Ngo, Tyler S. Bugg, Tadej Znidarcic, Jean-Marc Mojon, Glenna Gordon, Brenda Phipps, Amy Davidson, David Remnick, Nick Trautwein, Jake Silverstein, Ruth McDowall, Wunika Mukan, Chika Anekwe, Cristina Rivera, Malin Fezehai, Nneka Eze, Papa Omotayo, Joy Hepp, Krisanne Johnson, Elaine Braithwaite, Dayo Olopade, Jenna Wortham, Dana Hughes, Mansi Choksi, Lissa Minkel, Jiayang Fan, Laura Heaton, Mike Onyiego, May Jeong, Lauren Bohn, Alicia Patterson Foundation and Margaret Engel, New America, International Reporting Project, African Artists' Foundation and Azu Nwagbogu, Princeton in Africa, Carey Institute for Global Good, and, most of all, my family: Regina, David, David Jr., and George.